God's Miracles Among Us

True Stories of Healing, Hope, and the Power of God's Grace

Kate Cindel

Copyright

All rights reserved. No part of this book may be reproduced, stored in a retrieval system, or transmitted in any form or by any means, electronic, mechanical, photocopying, recording, or otherwise, without the prior written permission of the publisher, except for brief quotations used in reviews.

This book is a work of nonfiction. Any similarity to real persons, living or dead, is coincidental and not intended by the author.

© 2025 by Kate Cindel

Disclaimer

The stories, testimonies, and accounts presented in this book are shared for inspirational, educational, and faith-building purposes only. While every effort has been made to portray events accurately and respectfully, some details—including names, locations, timelines, and identifying characteristics—have been changed, condensed, or combined to protect the privacy of individuals and to enhance readability.

This book is not intended to diagnose, treat, cure, or prevent any physical, medical, emotional, or psychological condition. Readers should not use any information contained within these pages as a substitute for professional medical advice, diagnosis, or treatment. Always consult a qualified healthcare professional regarding any health concerns or decisions.

The author does not claim that miracles can be guaranteed, replicated, or predicted. The experiences described reflect the personal beliefs and interpretations of the individuals involved. Outcomes may differ from person to person, and no assurance is made regarding *similar results.*

Any opinions or perspectives expressed in this book are those of the author and contributors and do not represent the views of any medical institution, organization, or religious denomination referenced.

By reading this book, you acknowledge that you are responsible for your own decisions, beliefs, and interpretations and that the author and publisher are not liable for any direct or indirect consequences resulting from the use or misuse of the information presented herein.

Table of Contents

Introduction	7
Chapter One	**13**
The Child Who Wasn't Supposed to Live	13
Chapter Two	**27**
A Heart Restarted by Heaven	27
Chapter Three	**46**
"Get Up and Walk": A Recovery Beyond Science	46
Chapter Four	**67**
Pulled From Death's Grip	67
Chapter Five	**82**
The Invisible Nurse in the Emergency Room	82
Chapter Six	**101**
The Crash No One Survived — Except One	101
Chapter Seven	**116**
Fireproof Faith	116
Chapter Eight	**133**
Delivered Overnight	133
Chapter Nine	**147**
A Terminal Diagnosis That Disappeared	147
Chapter Ten	**163**
"I Forgave—and God Healed Me"	163
Chapter Eleven	**178**
The Missing Child Found Through Prayer	178
Chapter Twelve	**195**

A Whisper in the Storm	195
Chapter Thirteen	**210**
When God Sends the Right Person at the Right Time	210
Chapter Fourteen	**226**
Provision in the Final Hour	226
Chapter Fifteen	**243**
Everyday Miracles, Extraordinary God	243

Introduction

Some people say miracles are rare. Others insist they belong only to the pages of Scripture, reserved for ancient deserts, burning bushes, and seas that part at God's command. But if you listen closely—if you pay attention to the quiet corners of life—you will hear stories that challenge that belief. Stories whispered in hospital rooms, recounted in living rooms, shared in late-night phone calls, and told with trembling voices by people who know they should not be alive. Stories of the impossible becoming reality. Stories of God stepping into the ordinary days of ordinary people and leaving behind traces of His extraordinary power.

A recent global survey found that more than

half of adults believe they have experienced at least one miracle in their lifetime. They may not call it that. They may describe it as "luck," "timing," or "coincidence," because many people hesitate to attribute the unexplainable to God. Yet when pressed—when asked what they truly believe deep down—they admit there was something different about that moment, something sacred woven into the unexpected turn of events. Something that felt guided, protected, or intervened upon by a force greater than themselves. Behind those stories lies a truth humanity has sensed for centuries: miracles are not relics of the past. They are among us still.

What people often misunderstand is that miracles don't always roar. Some do—they shake entire families, stun medical experts, and leave communities speechless. A heart starts beating again after being still for far too long. A child with no chance of survival becomes the hope of an entire congregation. A diagnosis that was supposed to end a life vanishes before the next scan. These moments are breathtaking and undeniable, and they remind us that God's power has never weakened.

Yet just as real are the quieter miracles—the ones that slip through unnoticed unless we slow down long enough to see them. The near-misses that prevented tragedy. The internal voice that said "wait" at just the right moment. The stranger who appears out of nowhere with the exact words someone needed to hear. The dream that provides the direction a confused heart was crying out for. The peace that settles over someone in the middle of chaos—a peace that makes no sense unless it came from God Himself. These miracles may not make headlines, but they make all the difference in a life.

This book is a collection of those moments—large and small, dramatic and subtle, overwhelming and gently whispered. Each story carries its own weight, its own lesson, its own imprint of heaven touching earth. Together, they remind us that God is intimately involved in the details of our lives. He is not distant, silent, or idle. He is present—seeing, responding, guiding, protecting, healing, restoring, and comforting.

Some stories will make your heart race. Others

will bring tears to your eyes. Some will cause you to pause and reflect on your own journey, remembering moments that you once brushed off but now recognize as God's hand working quietly on your behalf. You may even discover miracles hidden in your own past—moments of protection, provision, or guidance you didn't recognize at the time.

What ties all of these accounts together is not the magnitude of the event, but the unmistakable fingerprint of God upon it. Whether He intervenes with breathtaking power or soft, unexpected timing, His presence leaves a mark that cannot be forgotten. These testimonies remind us that miracles are not only physical; they can be emotional, spiritual, relational, and deeply personal. Sometimes the most profound miracle is a heart softened, a soul restored, a fear lifted, or a burden replaced with strength.

And so, as you turn these pages, prepare to witness the God who still moves. The God who still heals. The God who still protects. The God who still whispers. The God who still answers. The God who knows every detail of your life and works through moments you may have never noticed. The God whose grace is not limited to ancient stories, but woven through every generation—including ours.

Miracles are not just in the extraordinary. They live in the everyday. They happen in light and in darkness, in crisis and in calm, in whispers and in wonders. They are everywhere, for those willing to see.

Chapter One

The Child Who Wasn't Supposed to Live

"Every three seconds, somewhere in the world, a mother cries out to God for her child."

It's a statistic often quoted in medical journals and faith-based studies alike, but numbers never fully prepare you for the moment that cry becomes your own voice trembling in a cold hospital hallway. That is where Emma and Jacob found themselves—hands shaking, hearts pounding, faces tight with fear—as they waited for a doctor to tell them whether their newborn son would live long enough to take another breath.

The pregnancy had been normal, uneventful even. Every ultrasound showed a strong heartbeat, steady growth, and the kind of reassuring notes obstetricians scribble into charts with confidence. Emma had followed every instruction, attended every appointment, and prayed every night with her hands resting on her belly. Jacob talked to the baby before bed, promising adventures, love, and a lifetime of protection. They had painted the nursery pale blue, assembled the crib, folded tiny clothes, and imagined the sound of newborn cries filling the quiet of their suburban home.

Nothing hinted at the storm that was coming.

He arrived just after 3 a.m., in a delivery room humming with fluorescent lights and the steady rhythm of monitors. His entrance into the world was strangely silent. No cry. No wail. No small, fragile protest of life. Emma remembers the way the room changed—how one nurse exchanged a glance with another, how the doctor pressed closer, how the soft murmur of congratulations faded into clipped medical instructions. She remembers Jacob's hand tightening around hers, the way his knuckles went white, the way he whispered, "It's okay. He's okay. He has to be."

But he wasn't. Not according to the monitors. Not according to the nurses who rushed the quiet baby toward a corner of the room Emma couldn't see. Not according to the doctor who said, with a voice tight and controlled, "Your son is having difficulty breathing. We need to take him immediately."

Emma barely caught a glimpse of him—small, still, wrapped loosely in a blanket—as he was wheeled away. She never imagined she would see her child for the first time from a distance of ten feet while he struggled for life.

In the NICU, they discovered the full scope of the crisis. His lungs were underdeveloped. His oxygen levels were dangerously low. His heart rhythm was unstable. The doctor assigned to his case, Dr. Ellis, had been in neonatology for twenty years; he had seen crises, losses, and rare triumphs. But even he struggled to mask his concern.

"He's very sick," he told them gently, the kind of tone doctors use when preparing a family for outcomes they never wanted to imagine. "We're doing everything we can."

Everything they could meant machines. Tubes.

IVs that disappeared into tiny, translucent veins. Electrodes taped to skin so fragile it bruised at the lightest touch. The NICU was filled with rhythmic beeps and the steady hiss of oxygen—sounds Emma would never forget for the rest of her life. She felt helpless, almost suspended between hope and despair, as if the world had narrowed down to the small glass box where her baby fought a silent war.

Jacob asked question after question, his voice steady but strained. He had always been the problem-solver, the planner, the man who believed every crisis could be approached logically. But logic had abandoned him. Nothing made sense. No answer brought comfort.

Emma held Jacob's arm as Dr. Ellis explained

the odds. They were not good. In fact, they were almost nonexistent.

"He's not responding to treatment," the doctor said quietly. "His lungs… they're simply not functioning the way they need to. And his heart—" He paused, collecting himself, as if reluctant to deliver the blow. "There's only so much we can do."

Emma heard the words, but they moved through her like distant noise. What she felt was something deeper—an ache that seemed to come from the center of her soul. She had carried him under her heart for nine months. She had dreamed of feeding him, holding him, singing him to sleep. And now she was being told she might have to say goodbye before she ever had the chance to say hello.

That night, they sat beside the incubator, watching the tiny chest rise and fall in uneven, fragile movements. Emma reached her fingers through the clear opening, touching the back of her baby's hand. It was warm, impossibly small, impossibly precious.

"Please," she whispered. "Please, God... don't take him. Not yet. Not like this."

Jacob bowed his head beside her. His prayer was quieter, but just as desperate. He wasn't a man who cried easily, but tears gathered in the corners of his eyes. "Lord," he whispered, "if You hear us, we need You now. We need You like we've never needed You before."

Nurses passed softly behind them, adjusting medications, checking monitors, speaking in hushed tones that carried both professionalism and compassion. The NICU was its own world—a place where time either rushed or slowed, where every second carried weight. In that space, parents learned how fragile life really was.

Around midnight, the baby's oxygen levels plummeted. The alarms erupted—a shrill, piercing sound that sent a jolt of terror through Emma's body. Nurses rushed forward. Dr. Ellis appeared almost instantly, as if the very sound of the alarm had summoned him.

"His heartbeat is dropping," a nurse said urgently.

"Prepare epinephrine," another commanded.

Emma felt Jacob pull her back, shielding her

from the commotion. She couldn't look away. Her baby, their baby, was turning a frightening shade of blue, like color was draining from him moment by moment.

"We're losing him," someone said. The words sliced through the air.

Emma broke. She didn't just cry—she pleaded. Her voice trembled, cracked, grew raw.

"God, please! Please don't let him die! Please save him!"

Jacob wrapped his arms around her, and together they wept prayers into the sterile air, prayers heavy enough to break the heart of heaven itself.

And then—something shifted.

Later, no one could fully explain what happened. Not the nurses. Not the doctor. Not even Jacob, who watched it unfold while holding his breath.

At the very moment Emma cried out, the monitors changed. The heart rhythm, which had been erratic and fading, steadied—slowly at first, then with more strength. The oxygen saturation, which had plunged into the red zone, climbed back up as if an unseen hand had intervened.

The room, moments before frantic, fell into a stunned silence.

"He's stabilizing," a nurse whispered, eyes wide.

Dr. Ellis stared at the monitor, then at the baby,

then back again. "This... this shouldn't be possible."

Emma and Jacob held each other, tears streaming, as their son's tiny chest rose in stronger, more consistent breaths. The color returned to his skin. The alarms quieted. The machines registered life, not decline.

They still remember the way Dr. Ellis stepped back from the bedside, shaking his head slowly—not in confusion, but in awe.

"I don't have an explanation for this," he said after several minutes. "Medically, nothing we did accounts for this turnaround. His lungs were failing. His heart was shutting down. And now..." He exhaled softly, overwhelmed. "Now he's... stable. Stronger. I've never seen anything like it."

That night became a dividing line in Emma and Jacob's lives. They walked into the NICU parents of a dying child. They left with the unmistakable sense that God had stepped into the room.

In the days that followed, the improvement continued. Each morning brought news better than the day before. The oxygen support decreased. Medications were slowly tapered. By the end of the week, their son opened his eyes for the first time—deep, steady, glistening with life that had nearly vanished. Emma wept as she held him against her chest, finally feeling the warmth of the baby she had begged God to save.

Jacob stood beside her, one hand resting on the tiny back, the other lifting a quiet prayer of gratitude. He didn't always understand the ways of God, but he knew what he saw. And what he saw was not coincidence.

Dr. Ellis visited often, each time marveling more. He never claimed it as a miracle outright—medicine rarely uses that word—but his silence, his lingering awe, his inability to explain… all of it told the truth his profession couldn't say aloud.

The day they finally carried their son out of the hospital, Emma held him close, memorizing every breath, every tiny movement. Jacob buckled him gently into the car seat, hands trembling—not with fear this time, but with reverence.

They had prayed from a place of desperation. God had answered from a place of power. Every beat of their son's heart was a reminder—grace had touched their lives, not in subtle ways but in ways so undeniable, even science had bowed its head in wonder.

Years later, Emma still recounts that night when fear battled hope, and hope won because God stepped into a glass box in a NICU and breathed life into a child who was never supposed to survive. Jacob still whispers prayers of gratitude over their son each night before bed, remembering how close they came to losing him. And their son—strong, laughing, full of life—grew up with a story that carried the fingerprint of heaven.

He wasn't supposed to live. But God had other

plans.

And that, Emma often says when she shares the story, is all the explanation they will ever need.

Chapter Two

A Heart Restarted by Heaven

"Every year, more than 356,000 people in the United States experience cardiac arrest outside a hospital. Only about 10% survive. Doctors call it one of the most unforgiving medical emergencies, because every passing minute without a heartbeat cuts the chance of survival by nearly 10%. But sometimes—despite the statistics, despite the science, despite every logical boundary—life surges back in a way no one can explain."

Michael Turner became one of those exceptions.

It happened on a quiet Thursday night in early spring, the kind of night where nothing feels unusual. Michael had just turned thirty-four, newly settled into a job he loved, newly engaged, and finally feeling like life had given him a sense of direction. He was the kind of person who seemed indestructible—the dependable friend who lifted everyone else's furniture, the coworker who never called in sick, the young man who ran three miles each morning without fail. He wasn't the kind anyone thought would collapse without warning.

That evening, he was sitting at the dinner table with his fiancée, Kara, reviewing the final guest list for their wedding. One moment he was laughing at her idea to shorten the reception playlist, and the next he paused, pressing a hand to his chest. She thought maybe he swallowed wrong or got choked up. She watched him try to take a breath—then another—and then the color drained from his face. His chair scraped the floor as he stood, only to crumple to the ground with a force that shook the table.

Kara screamed his name, expecting him to respond, but his eyes were open in a blank, distant stare she had never seen before. A stillness took over his face, the kind that terrifies even before you understand why. She grabbed her phone, shaking so badly that she could barely punch the numbers.

When the dispatcher asked if Michael was breathing, Kara hesitated. She wanted to say yes. She wanted to say anything that didn't make this moment real. But his chest didn't move. His lips began to cloud with blue.

She whispered, "No. He's not."

The dispatcher told her to start chest compressions immediately.

She had never learned CPR beyond what she saw in movies, but something in her snapped into action. Hands trembling, tears streaming, she interlocked her fingers and pushed down on Michael's chest with every ounce of strength she had. She counted out loud like the voice on the phone instructed, begging God with each number to please—please—let him breathe again.

When paramedics arrived, the living room had become an emergency zone. Furniture was pushed aside, a coffee table overturned, the wedding binder lying forgotten on the floor.

Kara stood back as the team lowered equipment around Michael, attaching patches to his chest, lifting his chin, assessing his pupils, working with a rhythm that was both frantic and precise. One paramedic counted compressions, another prepared the defibrillator, and a third delivered breaths through a bag mask.

Someone asked how long he had been down.

Kara answered, but her voice quivered in a way that made her words barely audible. Twelve minutes. Maybe thirteen. She wasn't sure. The minutes had blurred into each other, a terrifying mix of pleading and panic and the thud of her palms pushing against his sternum.

The lead paramedic glanced at another team member, a look not of surrender but of concern.

They all knew the unspoken truth: ten minutes without a heartbeat is devastating. Beyond that, hope fades quickly. Brain cells begin to die. Oxygen-starved organs shut down. Bodies slip into silence and rarely return. But the team refused to stop.

"Clear!"

The shock lifted Michael's chest slightly, then dropped him back to the floor. The monitor remained flat.

"Again. Charge it."

They tried a second time. Then a third.

Still no heartbeat.

Kara slid down the wall, burying her face in her hands, feeling the cold edge of dread pressing in so tightly she could hardly breathe. She listened to the paramedics speak in short, urgent exchanges, words she didn't fully understand but whose tone made her stomach twist.

One of them quietly said, "We need to transport."

They lifted Michael onto the stretcher, his arm falling limply to the side. Kara followed the ambulance in her car, gripping the steering wheel until her knuckles turned white, praying out loud the entire drive: "God, please. Please don't take him. Not like this. Not now. Not before our life even begins."

When she reached the hospital, they were already wheeling Michael into the trauma bay. She caught a glimpse through the doorway before a nurse stopped her. His body was still, motionless under the harsh fluorescent lights. A doctor stood over him, issuing orders with clipped urgency. Nurses moved around him with syringes, lines, and the mechanical chest compressor positioned above his body.

A nurse guided Kara to a nearby chair and asked her gently if she needed water. Kara shook her head, her lips trembling. She didn't want water. She wanted Michael to open his eyes. She wanted to hear his voice. She wanted this nightmare to end.

The medical team administered epinephrine, restarted compressions, attempted another defibrillation. But as the minutes passed, the room took on a different tone—still determined, still fighting, but heavy with the weight of reality.

He had now been without a heartbeat for more than twenty-five minutes.

A resident whispered to the attending, "Do you want to call it?"

The attending didn't answer immediately. He looked at the monitor, at Michael's still face, at the shaking hands of the nurses who refused to give up. Then he looked toward the doorway, where Kara sat with tears streaking her cheeks, gripping her engagement ring like an anchor.

"Give me one more round," the attending said.

They pushed another dose of medication. Reset the defibrillator. Prepared for what was likely their final attempt.

Kara slid from her chair to her knees, her hands clasped, her forehead pressed to the floor. Her voice broke as she whispered, "God, if You are here... if You see him... please. Bring him back. I can't do life without him. I can't. Please breathe into him again."

Something shifted in the room then. It wasn't dramatic or loud—not a gust of wind, not a flash of light—but a quiet, noticeable change in the atmosphere. Nurses later described it as a stillness that replaced the panic, a calm that washed over the tense urgency. No one spoke for a moment. It felt as though the room itself paused.

The attending placed the defibrillator paddles one more time and nodded. "Clear."

Michael's body jolted.

The monitor flickered.

A faint blip appeared—tiny, weak, almost imperceptible.

Then another.

And then, impossibly, a rhythm began to form. Slow at first, wavering, but undeniably present.

One of the nurses gasped. Another placed her hands over her mouth. A third, who had spent twenty years in emergency medicine, stepped back as tears filled her eyes.

"He's back," the attending said softly.

Kara looked up, unable to process the words. A nurse ran out of the trauma bay, her expression disbelieving. "He has a pulse," she whispered.

Kara's legs felt weak as she rushed inside. She saw Michael's chest rising slightly under the ventilator, a sign that life—real life—had returned where none should have been possible. Her sobs broke free, raw and loud, as she reached for his hand.

The attending leaned toward her. "We did everything we could. But this…" He glanced at the monitor again, at the fragile line drawing peaks where there had only been flatness. "This is beyond what medicine explains."

They transferred Michael to the ICU, where he remained unconscious. The doctors warned Kara and his family that the lack of oxygen could mean severe brain damage. They said the next twenty-four hours were critical. They said they couldn't predict anything. They said they would do everything possible, but they couldn't guarantee how much of Michael would return—if any.

Kara stayed by his bedside, holding his hand, reading Scripture over him, praying without ceasing. His parents arrived and joined her, their voices quiet but steady as they whispered prayers for healing.

Hours passed. Machines hummed. Nurses checked vitals. Doctors reviewed charts. Kara watched every rise and fall of Michael's chest, clinging to hope even as fear nipped at the edges of her mind.

Just after sunrise, Michael stirred.

It was small—a twitch in his fingers, barely there—but Kara saw it. She stood so fast her chair toppled backward. She leaned close.

Michael's eyelids fluttered.

Then, slowly, painfully, he opened his eyes.

Kara choked on a breath she didn't know she'd been holding. She pressed a trembling hand to his cheek. "Michael? Can you hear me?"

He blinked a few times, confused, groggy, fighting to understand. His lips parted just enough for her to hear the faint whisper:

"Kara?"

Tears streamed down her face.

A nurse hurried in, saw what was happening, and stepped back into the hallway calling for the attending. When he arrived and assessed Michael's responses, he shook his head in astonishment.

"He knows where he is," the attending said. "His memory's intact. His neurological function looks… unbelievably good."

He lowered his voice. "This should not be possible."

Over the next few days, Michael improved rapidly. Doctors ordered test after test, shaking their heads as each one came back better than expected. His heart regained normal function. His brain scans showed no signs of hypoxic injury. His speech, coordination, and cognition were intact.

Every nurse who cared for him said the same thing: they had never seen anything like it.

The attending visited Michael after he was

transferred to a regular room. He placed a hand on the bed rail and spoke quietly.

"Michael, I've been in medicine a long time. I've seen some remarkable things. But what happened to you..." He paused, searching for words grounded in truth, not routine. "There's no medical explanation for the recovery you've made. Your fiancée prayed over you in a way I'll never forget. And something changed in that room. I don't say this lightly, but what happened... it's a miracle."

Michael looked at Kara, then back at the doctor, emotion swelling in his chest. He didn't know how to respond except with gratitude—gratitude to God, gratitude to the people who fought for him, gratitude for a second chance he would never take for granted.

When Michael finally left the hospital, the staff lined the hall to clap for him. Some smiled. Some cried. All of them felt they had witnessed something extraordinary, something that defied the boundaries of medicine.

Michael squeezed Kara's hand, promising himself silently that he would never forget the night his heart was restarted by something greater than human effort.

In the quiet days that followed, he found a new rhythm in life. He woke each morning aware that breath itself was a gift. He told his story to anyone who asked—but always with the same certainty in his voice: "I wasn't brought back just so I could keep living. I was brought back so I could live differently."

His experience changed everything—his faith, his priorities, his understanding of purpose. It changed Kara too, deepening her confidence that God still moves in ways far beyond human reason. His parents, the medical team, even strangers who heard the story felt something stir in them as well—a reminder that heaven still touches earth in moments that can't be rationalized away.

Michael Turner became one of the few who defied every medical prediction, every grim statistic, every expected outcome. His heart had stopped. His life had slipped away. Science had reached its limit.

But grace had not.

And in that gap—where human ability ends and

God's power begins—the impossible became real.

Chapter Three

"Get Up and Walk": A Recovery Beyond Science

"More than 5 million people around the world live with paralysis, yet every year doctors record cases of sudden, unexplainable recoveries that defy everything medical science expects." Those statistics from the Christopher & Dana Reeve Foundation came back to Daniel's mind months after the day his life changed forever—the day he heard a sound like a branch snapping, felt a bolt of pain shoot through his back, and collapsed on a quiet stretch of road with no ability to move his legs. He had read the number somewhere in a magazine once, never imagining he would become part of it. But the moment his body hit

the ground, the moment the burning pain shot through his spine and turned into a heavy, dead numbness, he knew something had gone terribly wrong.

There had been nothing remarkable about the morning. He'd woken before dawn, brewed his coffee, and stepped outside to take a run as he always did. The sky was washed in pale blue, the kind of morning that made you breathe a little deeper. Daniel was only twenty-nine, healthy, athletic, full of plans he'd never say out loud because life felt too solid, too predictable, to imagine it could change. He'd never feared his body, never questioned its ability to carry him. But a single step on loose gravel, a slip, and a fall twisted his spine in a way no one could have foreseen. He tried to stand, but his legs wouldn't respond. It felt as if they'd disappeared, as if they were no longer part of him at all.

A motorist found him minutes later, lying sideways on the shoulder of the road, conscious but terrified. He couldn't move. Not a toe, not a foot, nothing. The woman who stopped called 911 while trying to keep him calm, but Daniel could see it in her eyes—the fear, the uncertainty, the silent questions. He felt cold despite the rising sun. When the paramedics arrived and lifted him onto the stretcher, he felt the pressure of their hands but nothing at all below his waist. No tingling. No sensation. Just emptiness.

At the hospital the tests came quickly—X-rays, CT scans, MRIs—images splashed across monitors showing a spinal cord with swelling around the lower thoracic vertebrae. The doctor's face was controlled, but not calm. Daniel remembered every detail: the blue tie, the faint smell of antiseptic on his gloves, the way he paused for one extra second before speaking. "There's spinal trauma," he said. "Significant swelling. We can treat the inflammation and stabilize the injury, but you need to prepare for the possibility that movement may not return."

The words echoed and re-echoed. Daniel felt like he was watching himself from above, seeing his life fold inward while the room around him kept moving. Machines beeped. Nurses walked past his curtain. The world continued. But his had stopped. When they finally left him alone to process the news, he stared at the ceiling tiles and tried to make his toes move. He could feel nothing—not an ache, not a tingle, not even a sense of where his legs should be. It was as if they belonged to someone else.

His family arrived within an hour. His mother's tears came first, then the quiet determination in his father's voice as he said, "We're going to get through this." Daniel didn't respond at first. He didn't know how. He'd been strong his whole life, the kind of man friends described as steady, grounded, dependable. But lying in that bed, unable to move, unable to feel anything below the waist, he felt small, powerless, broken. His sister stepped close and held his hand. She prayed softly, words trembling but sincere. Daniel closed his eyes and listened, not yet ready to speak to God, but unable to stop hearing His name.

The first night was the hardest. Every time he closed his eyes he relived the fall, the snap of pain, the sudden numbness. Nurses turned him every few hours to prevent pressure sores. Physical therapists evaluated him and charted muscle responses that didn't exist. Doctors explained treatment plans involving steroids, time, and cautious optimism. But optimism was difficult when he stared at his still, lifeless legs.

By the third day, the swelling had not improved. A specialist reviewed the scans and shook his head. "We will keep monitoring," he said, "but there are injuries the body does not reverse. What you regain, if anything, will depend on

God and biology." Daniel heard both parts of the sentence, but the first part struck deeper. He had grown up in church, had spent his childhood learning Scriptures about healing, deliverance, miracles—but as an adult he had drifted. Not in rebellion, but in quiet neglect. God was still a name he respected, but not Someone he turned to unless life demanded it.

Life was demanding it now.

On the fourth day, his pastor visited. He sat beside Daniel's bed and spoke gently, telling him stories of others who had survived accidents, of people who had regained movement, of prayers answered long after hope was gone. Daniel listened, but the seed of faith hadn't yet broken through the concrete of fear. He nodded out of politeness, not belief. He thanked him for coming, but he didn't pray with conviction. Not yet.

That evening the church held a prayer meeting for him. His mother streamed it from her phone so Daniel could hear. Dozens of voices rose at once—friends, elders, people he hadn't seen in years—calling on God to restore what had been lost. Something inside Daniel cracked—not loudly, but unmistakably. Tears came unexpectedly, sliding across his face and down into his hair. He felt vulnerable, but strangely comforted.

The next morning, something shifted. Not in his body, but in the atmosphere around him. Daniel felt different inside—tired of fear, tired of imagining a future trapped in a wheelchair, tired of believing that the story was already over. A nurse came in to check his vitals, and he whispered, "Can you give me a moment?" She nodded and stepped out.

Daniel stared at the ceiling once more, but this time his heart was open. "God," he whispered, "I don't know what to pray. I don't know what to expect. I don't even know what I believe right now. But if You're still with me… if You still work miracles… if this isn't the end… please help me."

He didn't pray long. He didn't know what else to say. But the moment he finished, the room felt lighter—not warm, not glowing, just… lighter. Peace crept into the cracks of his fear like sunlight touching a dark room for the first time.

That afternoon his family came again. His mother stood at the foot of the bed and said, "We want to pray with you. Not around you. With you." Daniel nodded. They joined hands—his mother on one side, his father on the other, his sister resting her hand gently on his shin though he could not feel it. Their voices blended into one prayer, steady and resolute, speaking life over dead nerves, strength over injured tissue, hope over despair. Daniel did something he hadn't done since childhood—he prayed aloud with them.

As they prayed, Daniel felt a warmth in his chest. Not hot, not burning—just warm, like someone had placed a hand inside him and was comforting him from the inside out. His breathing deepened. His shoulders relaxed. And then, faint as a whisper, something stirred.

At first he thought he imagined it. A sensation like a feather brushing the bottom of his right foot. His eyes flew open. His sister was still praying softly, her hand resting lightly on his motionless leg. He held his breath. There it was again—a faint, almost distant tingling. Not movement. Not pain. Just—feeling.

"Mom," he whispered.

She continued praying.

"Mom," he said again, louder this time. She opened her eyes, startled.

"I felt something."

Her breath caught. "What do you mean?"

"My foot. I felt something on my foot."

His father stepped back in disbelief. His mother covered her mouth with both hands. His sister began crying before a single word could escape her throat. They stared at him, waiting, trembling.

Daniel focused every bit of attention he had on his foot. He tried to move his toes. Nothing. He tried again. Still nothing. He closed his eyes and whispered, "Lord… if this is You, don't stop."

The tingling grew stronger—not much, but enough to make him gasp. It spread slowly, rising from the foot to the ankle, like a current traveling up a long-dead wire searching for a connection. Daniel clenched the bedsheets, overwhelmed. His family didn't speak; they didn't dare interrupt what was happening.

A nurse walked in during the moment and froze. She saw Daniel's face, saw the tears running freely, saw his family staring at his legs with stunned silence. "Everything okay?" she asked, stepping toward the bed.

Daniel swallowed. "Can you... touch the bottom of my foot?"

She hesitated. Daniel's mother nodded desperately. The nurse pulled off a glove, reached down, and pressed her finger against the sole of Daniel's right foot.

He twitched.

Not a full movement. Just a flicker. A tiny, involuntary jerk. But it was movement—movement that wasn't supposed to be possible.

The nurse gasped. "I saw that. I saw that! Hold on—let me get the doctor."

Within minutes a team of physicians crowded the room. They ran sensory tests, reflex tests, nerve stimulation, pinpricks. Each time they tested him, Daniel felt something—maybe faint, maybe inconsistent, but undeniably real.

By the next morning, the tingling had reached both ankles. Later that afternoon, sensation crawled up past his calves. The spinal swelling, once unchanged, had decreased more in twelve hours than in the previous four days combined. The medical team couldn't explain it. They tried. They used terms like "unexpected," "unusual," "inconsistent with initial prognosis," but none of their words captured what everyone in the room knew deep down.

Something was happening that medicine had no formula for.

Daniel began physical therapy the moment sensation reached his knees. The therapists were cautious, explaining that feeling didn't automatically mean strength. They warned him not to expect rapid progress. Daniel listened politely, but inside he felt a courage he hadn't felt since the fall. Not denial—confidence. A quiet assurance that God was doing something far beyond human expectation.

On the eighth day in the hospital, they fitted him with braces to support his legs while they tested his ability to bear a small amount of weight. Daniel gripped the parallel bars tightly as the physical therapist positioned his feet on the floor.

"Don't be discouraged if nothing happens today," she said. "This is just about seeing where you are."

Daniel nodded, but his heart was pounding.

His mother stood near the door with her hands over her heart. His father looked like he wasn't breathing at all. His sister held her phone with trembling fingers, recording the moment because she believed—truly believed—something extraordinary was going to happen.

"Okay," the therapist said softly. "Let's see if you can shift your weight."

Daniel inhaled. Slowly, gently, he tried to lean forward.

His right leg trembled.

The therapist froze. Daniel tried again, putting more intention, more faith, more trust into the movement.

His knee bent.

Gasps filled the room. Daniel's chest tightened with emotion. He gripped the bars harder, focused all his energy on his legs, and whispered under his breath, "Lord, help me."

He shifted again.

His left foot pressed against the floor—not firmly, not fully, but enough to take a fraction of his weight.

"Daniel," the therapist whispered, voice shaking, "you're doing it."

He couldn't answer. Tears blurred his vision.

His throat tightened. He felt the strength rising slowly through his legs, like someone reconnecting a series of wires that had long been broken.

Then, without warning, his right leg straightened.

His mother let out a sob. His father pressed his fist to his mouth, blinking hard. The therapist could not hide the disbelief on her face.

Daniel took a deep breath, lifted his left leg, and placed it forward.

A step.

Small. Unsteady. Supported. But a step—his step.

A sound filled the room then—not a shout, not a

cheer, but the raw, holy cry of people witnessing something they knew they could never explain. Daniel felt the weight of the moment settle into his heart like a vow. He wasn't walking because of medicine alone. He wasn't walking because his body was strong. He was walking because God had touched what human hands could not reach.

He took another step.

And another.

Slow. Shaking. Tear-filled.

But walking.

Each step felt like a declaration that the story was not determined by prognosis or by fear. The room blurred as tears streamed freely. His mother was on her knees praying, thanking God with every breath. His father reached out and touched Daniel's back, unable to speak. The therapist wiped her eyes, whispering, "I've never seen anything like this."

Daniel wasn't thinking about the fall anymore. Or the statistics. Or the predictions that said movement might never return. He was thinking about the prayer whispered in a room that felt too quiet. The hands that held his. The voices that rose for him. The moment sensation returned like a spark waiting for ignition. The warmth that flooded his chest just before everything changed.

And he kept walking—one trembling step after another—knowing with absolute certainty that what he was experiencing was more than recovery. More than science. More than the best doctors could explain.

He was living a miracle.

Chapter Four

Pulled From Death's Grip

"Every year, an estimated 236,000 people drown worldwide. Less than 1% of those submerged longer than ten minutes ever return to life without brain damage."

The statistic itself feels like a verdict—cold, final, and unmoving. Numbers don't cry. Numbers don't tremble. Numbers don't kneel beside the lifeless body of someone they love and whisper, *Please, God... not yet.* But people do. And on a freezing winter afternoon, when ice covered Lake Merrin like a glass shield, one of those impossible moments broke the rules of science, logic, and survival. It's the kind of event that refuses to be explained, the kind that physicians discuss quietly in break rooms, shaking their heads because there is simply no medical language for what they witnessed. It's the kind of moment that belongs only in a book titled *God's Miracles Among Us*, because no other explanation truly fits.

It began with the sound of laughter—three teenagers racing toward the frozen shoreline like it was an open invitation. The sun sat low, turning the ice into a sheet of dull silver. None of them noticed the thin patches. None of them felt the danger underneath their feet. They were chasing freedom, winter air, and the boldness that comes with being young and invincible. Seventeen-year-old Caleb Hart was the tallest of them, the one who dared farther, the one who believed nothing bad could happen on a day that felt so ordinary.

The air snapped cold around them as they slid across the surface. Caleb's shoes skidded, his balance tipped, and then—without warning—the world beneath him gave way. One moment he was laughing. The next he dropped straight down with a violent crack that echoed across the lake. A splash swallowed his scream, and then the water closed over him.

In an instant, everything changed.

The other boys froze, wide-eyed, as the ice fractured around the hole. Their voices bounced across the lake—shouts of terror, pleas for help, the raw panic of helplessness. Caleb fought upward, his hands scraping desperately against the jagged edges of ice that crumbled under his fingers. The water didn't just bite; it seized him. Cold so sharp it felt alive wrapped around his chest and stole his breath. He tried to gasp, but the water slammed into his throat, into his lungs, into the very place breath was supposed to be. The lake swallowed him as if it had hands.

His friends threw themselves forward, crawling on their stomachs to distribute their weight, stretching as far as they could. "Grab my arm!" one of them yelled, but Caleb was slipping under again. The current beneath the ice dragged him, twisting his body away from the opening. He couldn't see them anymore. The world went dark, quiet, and terrifyingly still.

Under the ice, sound disappeared. Sight disappeared. The only thing left was cold—cold that burned, cold that silenced thought, cold that whispered in a voice almost gentle: *Let go.*

He tried to fight it, but consciousness was dissolving. The icy water slowed everything—his heart, his breathing, his ability to understand what was happening. Panic gave way to a strange, sinking calm. The world above grew dimmer, muffled, unreachable, and then everything faded.

On the surface, chaos erupted. Someone from shore saw the boys waving frantically and called 911. By the time the first rescue truck screamed into the parking lot, Caleb had been underwater for more than ten minutes. Statistics said he should already be gone. Rescuers hacked at the ice, plunging poles into the water, sweeping in wide arcs. Shouts overlapped: "I think I felt something!" "No pulse!" "Move—let me get in!" The urgency in their voices didn't come from protocol. It came from hope slipping through their fingers.

They finally found him twenty feet from where he fell in—face down, motionless, limbs pale and slack. When they lifted him from the water, his skin had turned a frightening shade of grayish blue. His eyes were partially open, unfocused. His chest didn't rise. His lips held the color of something long gone from life.

Paramedics began CPR immediately on the ice itself. One counted compressions with a voice so steady it felt inhuman. Another forced air into Caleb's lungs, watching helplessly as his chest remained stubbornly still. The cold had slowed everything to the edge of death. His heart wasn't beating. His lungs weren't drawing breath. His body temperature had plummeted to levels considered incompatible with life.

They loaded him into the ambulance. CPR continued. Another round of epinephrine. No response. Another. Nothing. His friends watched from the shoreline, trembling, hugging themselves, whispering through sobs that this couldn't be happening. One of them kept saying, "God, please… please… please…" as if the repetition alone might force heaven's attention.

At the hospital, the ER team worked with mechanical precision. Wires attached. Machines clicked. Monitors beeped with flat indifference. Caleb had been without a pulse for nearly an hour. His pupils didn't react to light. His organs were shutting down from prolonged oxygen deprivation. A nurse whispered to the attending physician, "There's nothing left to do."

They were moments away from calling time of death.

And then Caleb's mother walked into the room.

She didn't scream. She didn't collapse. She stepped forward with a calmness that didn't match the moment. Her hands trembled slightly, but her eyes burned with determination. She reached for her son's foot—cold, stiff, lifeless—and whispered a prayer so soft the staff barely heard her.

"God, I know You're here. I know You're the One who gives breath. Give it back to him. Please... I'm asking You to return my son."

A nurse later said the room felt different when she prayed—as if the air thickened with presence. Another said she felt chills, not from fear, but from something she couldn't name. No alarms were sounding. No machines were responding. But something shifted.

Less than ten seconds after she prayed, a faint electrical blip appeared on the cardiac monitor.

The team stiffened. The attending leaned closer. Another blip. Then a weak but undeniable rhythm. Someone shouted, "We have a heartbeat!" Nurses rushed to adjust equipment. A respiratory therapist repositioned the ventilator. The room, moments before preparing for death, erupted into urgent movement.

Caleb's pulse strengthened—slowly at first,

then steadily. His chest rose with mechanical breaths, but now his heart supported the effort. A nurse touched her hand to her mouth and whispered, "This doesn't happen."

They moved him to intensive care. His survival was unlikely. His survival *with brain function* was considered impossible. Doctors warned the family to prepare for the worst. They explained the medical facts carefully, gently. No oxygen for this long meant severe brain injury, if he lived at all. Caleb might never wake up. If he did, he'd likely be in a vegetative state.

But his mother refused fear. She sat beside his bed, her hand wrapped around his cold fingers, whispering prayers through the night. "God, I believe You didn't bring him back for nothing. Finish what You started."

Hours passed. Machines hummed. Nurses checked vitals. And then, as dawn broke, Caleb's eyelids twitched. A soft sound escaped his throat. The nurse leaned forward. His fingers moved. His eyes blinked again—with focus, with purpose.

They called the doctor. More staff poured into the room. Caleb looked confused, exhausted, but awake. Nobody expected words—not with the swelling, not with the trauma—but he whispered, "Mom?"

It was a single word. A small sound. But it shattered every medical expectation.

In the days that followed, he regained memory, speech, and full neurological function. The MRI showed no brain damage. His organs stabilized.

His heart regained strength. The medical team reviewed the records repeatedly, baffled. Some admitted openly that there was no explanation. One doctor said quietly to Caleb's mother, "This isn't medicine. This is something... beyond us."

Caleb left the hospital three weeks later, walking on his own, smiling, laughing—alive in every sense of the word.

But the miracle didn't end there.

Caleb's life began to reflect a purpose marked long before that icy fall. He spoke at schools, sharing his story. He visited drowning prevention programs, encouraging families to learn rescue skills. He prayed with others facing hopeless diagnoses. His survival became more than an event—it became a calling. People who had never believed in miracles before pointed to him as evidence that God still intervenes.

He often said he didn't remember much from under the ice—only a sense of surrender. But he did remember the moment he woke in the hospital and realized he was alive. He said it felt like warmth rushing through him, something deeper than heat, something that filled every part of him with strength.

"It felt," he said once in an interview, "like someone breathed for me when I couldn't. Like God put life back inside me."

Years later, one of the paramedics who helped pull him from the lake admitted that every time she retold the story, she felt the same chills she

81

felt that day. "I've worked in emergency rescue for twenty years," she said. "I've seen tragedy. I've seen miracles too—but nothing like that. That wasn't luck. That wasn't biology. That was God."

Caleb is the kind of story mothers whisper to their children at night when they're afraid. The kind pastors tell when someone feels God has forgotten them. The kind that keeps prayer alive in hospital hallways where hope seems absent. Because when someone is pulled from death's grip after an hour without a heartbeat, and when that person walks out of the hospital with no damage, no deficits, no explanation, the event demands to be recognized as something sacred.

Caleb doesn't call himself special. He doesn't call himself chosen. But he does say that God clearly had a reason for returning his breath. And whenever someone asks why he survived when so many don't, he answers with quiet honesty:

"I don't know why God chose to save me. But since He did, I'm going to live like every breath is borrowed from Him."

And every time he says it, those who hear him can feel the weight of the miracle—real, undeniable, and still echoing across the surface of a frozen lake that once should have been his final resting place, but instead became the place where God's power brought a lifeless boy back into the world of the living.

Chapter Five

The Invisible Nurse in the Emergency Room

"More than 130 million people walk through emergency room doors in the United States every year. Nurses and doctors rush, alarms blare, and seconds determine the line between life and death. Yet, from time to time, staff report something that doesn't fit any chart, code, or clinical protocol: a helper who appears out of nowhere, knows exactly what to do, and is gone before anyone can ask their name."

It was a statistic Maria Hernandez had read months before her shift in the trauma wing that Thursday evening. At the time, she dismissed such stories as stress-fed illusions—figments created by exhausted minds running on caffeine and adrenaline. But the night Samuel Price was wheeled into her ER, half-conscious and bleeding heavily, that statistic would take on a meaning she could never erase.

It started at 7:46 p.m.—two minutes before the shift-change lull. Maria was double-checking the medication logs when the bay doors slammed open and paramedics rushed in with a man in his mid-forties. He had been hit head-on by a truck while turning off a rural highway. His carotid pulse was thready, his skin pale, and a deep wound along his left abdomen pulsed with dark blood each time his heart struggled.

"We're losing him," one of the paramedics muttered. "BP's crashing."

Maria moved in fast. "Bay 3. Prep for massive transfusion protocol." Everyone snapped into motion—gloves on, masks up, carts wheeled in with metallic clatter. The sterile lights above flickered as Samuel's gurney rolled under them. Someone shouted for O-negative. Another shouted for a crash cart.

For a moment the room vibrated with overlapping voices, slamming drawers, beeping alarms, and the muffled sounds of Samuel trying to breathe through the pain. Chaos was nothing new to Maria. Years in emergency medicine had taught her to function like a metronome—steady, focused, one task at a time, no matter how loud the world became around her.

But even she felt the tension rising. The wound

wouldn't stop bleeding. The sutures weren't holding. The doctor on call, Dr. Bell, was still several minutes away, stuck in traffic after a multi-car pileup that had clogged the northbound expressway. The trauma surgeon was still finishing a procedure upstairs.

They were short-staffed. They were out of time. And Samuel's blood pressure dipped another ten points.

"Maria—he's crashing!" one of the techs yelled as the monitor screamed its shrill alarm.

She tightened the abdominal clamp, but her hands trembled. "Come on, stay with us," she whispered through clenched teeth.

That was the moment the air shifted.

Maria didn't notice him walk in. She couldn't

tell if the door opened, or if he'd already been standing there unnoticed among the frantic flood of bodies. But suddenly a man was beside her—calm, steady, soft-spoken. She turned her head, startled. He wore a simple pale-blue scrub top, clean and pressed, with no hospital logo, badge, or name tag. His presence was so quiet it almost seemed unreal, like he didn't disturb the space he entered.

"I can help," he said gently.

Maria blinked at him, caught between urgency and confusion. There were no float nurses scheduled tonight. She knew every face on the roster; she had attended the briefing. This man wasn't part of it.

But before she could ask anything, he moved

with precise confidence, placing two fingers against Samuel's neck as if he could read something deeper than a pulse. Then he looked directly at Maria with eyes that radiated an unusual certainty.

"You need to adjust the clamp higher," he said. "A vessel is torn right above where you're holding."

"But the ultrasound—" she began.

"There's no time. Trust me."

His voice wasn't forceful, yet it carried a weight that made the room feel still. Even the chaos seemed to pause around him. Maria didn't know why she listened—protocol demanded imaging confirmation—but something in his tone steadied her trembling hands. She slid the clamp up several millimeters and tightened.

Almost instantly, the bleeding slowed.

The tech staring at the monitor gasped. "Pulse stabilizing. Pressure's rising!"

The man nodded once, as if this was the outcome he already expected. Then he turned to the nurse nearest the IV stand. "Increase fluids. He'll tolerate it. But not more than a liter before the surgeon gets here."

"Yes, sir," she responded before realizing she'd never seen him before.

Maria tried again. "Who are you? Which department—?"

But the man moved to Samuel's side, placing a hand gently on his shoulder. There was something peaceful in the gesture—something grounding. Samuel's breathing, strained and uneven moments ago, softened. His eyelids fluttered. His clenched jaw relaxed.

"It's not his time," the man murmured, barely audible over the hum of machines. "He has things left to do."

Maria felt a chill ripple across her skin. She didn't understand how he could say that with such certainty. But the fear she had fought for the last ten minutes ebbed, replaced by an unexpected sense of order. The room felt warmer somehow. Brighter.

A moment later, Dr. Bell burst into the bay. "What've we got?"

Maria stepped aside to summarize. "Severe

laceration, major blood loss, but pressure's stabilizing after repositioning the clamp."

Dr. Bell glanced at the monitor, brows lifted. "That was the right move. Good call."

"It wasn't mine," Maria said, turning to gesture toward the man—

—but he wasn't there.

She scanned the entire ER bay. The corner by the supply cabinet. The sink near the crash cart. The entry door. The hallway beyond.

Nothing. No movement. No pale-blue scrubs.

He had vanished as quietly as he had appeared.

"Where'd he go?" one of the techs asked, craning his neck.

"Who?" Dr. Bell asked.

"The nurse," Maria said. "Tall, dark hair, blue top, no badge. He helped clamp the vessel."

Dr. Bell frowned. "There's no nurse like that scheduled tonight."

"I saw him," Maria insisted. "He was right here."

"So did I," said the tech at the IV stand. "He told me how much fluid to run."

A third staff member nodded slowly. "He helped hold pressure before the clamp adjustment."

Dr. Bell opened his mouth to respond but froze, unsettled. "We'll figure it out later. Right now, prep for OR."

The next ten minutes moved in a blur. The surgical team arrived, Samuel was stabilized enough for transport, and the gurney rolled out of the trauma bay. Maria followed the team to the elevator, watching the man they had fought so hard to save disappear into the sterile hallway beyond.

When she returned to Bay 3, the room was already being cleaned, the floors scrubbed, the surfaces wiped down. The adrenaline faded, leaving her with one bewildering question: Who was that man?

She walked to the charge desk. "Can you check the staffing logs again? Maybe someone volunteered from another wing?"

The charge nurse pulled up the roster. "I

promise you, Maria, no one matches that description. No one."

"What about from ICU?"

"No."

"OR suite?"

"No."

"Transport?"

"No one."

Maria leaned against the counter, stunned. "I don't understand."

The charge nurse hesitated. "This isn't the first time staff have reported… someone. Usually during critical cases. Always when things look impossible."

"You're saying this is a thing?"

"I'm saying you're not the first person who's asked that question in this building."

Maria pressed a hand to her forehead, replaying the moment the man had appeared. The steady eyes. The calm tone. The certainty in his words. The way fear had melted the second he spoke.

There was something else too—something she hadn't consciously registered until now. When he stood beside her, she realized she hadn't heard him breathe. Not a single inhale or exhale. His presence had been weightless, like he belonged to the room but not to the physical world.

The next day, after Samuel returned from surgery in stable condition, his wife, Caroline, arrived. She was pale from lack of sleep, trembling as she approached the nurses' station.

"Is he going to live?" she asked, her voice thin.

"He's recovering well," Maria said. "He's very strong."

Tears flooded Caroline's eyes. "You don't understand. On the drive here, I prayed like I've never prayed in my life. I begged God not to take him. I said, 'Lord, send someone to help him until the doctors can get there. Don't leave him alone.'"

Maria stared at her.

Caroline continued, voice shaking. "I asked God to send an angel. I didn't mean it literally. I meant… someone who knew what to do. Someone who could keep him alive until the surgeons could help him."

The air between them felt charged, heavy with meaning.

"Caroline," Maria whispered, "can I ask you something? Did your husband have any relatives in the medical field? Anyone who might have come in with him? A friend? A coworker?"

"No," Caroline said, confused. "Why?"

Maria hesitated. "Because there was a man who helped us last night. But he wasn't on staff. He wasn't on any roster. And after he helped us… he disappeared."

Caroline pressed a hand to her mouth. "What did he look like?"

Maria described him as best she could.

Caroline's expression shifted into something Maria couldn't decipher—half awe, half trembling disbelief. "Samuel told me something once," she whispered. "He said that when he was a child, he nearly drowned in a neighbor's pool. Someone pulled him out. A man in a pale-blue shirt. His parents never found out who he was. They thought it was a passerby. But Samuel swore the man looked… just like that."

Maria felt goosebumps rise along her arms.

Caroline stepped closer, her voice lower. "I think God has been sending the same protector his whole life."

Maria swallowed hard. "You think he was an angel?"

"I don't know what else to think," Caroline said, tears spilling over. "But I know I asked God for help at that exact moment. And someone came."

Later that evening, as Maria walked past the now-quiet trauma bay, she paused at the doorway. The same sterile lights that had shone on chaos the night before now illuminated a spotless room. Yet she could almost feel the echo of the calm that had entered with the mysterious man.

She stepped inside and looked at the spot where he had stood—hands steady, voice unwavering, eyes filled with something she still couldn't explain. She replayed the scene in her mind: the sudden slowing of blood loss, the rise in Samuel's pulse, the shift in the room's atmosphere.

There had been no fear in the man. No rush. No hesitation. Only certainty and peace.

She thought of Caroline's prayer.

She thought of Samuel's childhood story.

She thought of the countless unresolved reports her charge nurse hinted at.

She thought of how the man had looked at Samuel—not at his wound, but at his face—as if he knew him. As if he had known him for years.

Maria exhaled slowly.

Some miracles happen with sirens blazing and doctors shouting orders. Some arrive through medicine, skill, and science. And some—rare, quiet, unexplainable—come in the form of a stranger who steps into the chaos, brings peace, restores life…

…and disappears before anyone can thank him.

She stood there alone, the hum of overhead lights soft and steady, and let the truth settle in her heart.

What happened in Bay 3 wasn't coincidence. It wasn't random. And it wasn't human.

Something holy had stepped into that room.

Something sent.

Someone sent.

And though she would never know his name, she knew one thing with absolute certainty:

God had answered a desperate prayer in the most extraordinary way.

Chapter Six

The Crash No One Survived — Except One

"Most fatal accidents happen within five miles of home." It's a statistic people often repeat without thinking deeply about it. But for Daniel Carter, it became a chilling reality on a warm evening in late August, when a road he'd driven hundreds of times suddenly became the setting of a story no one in his town would ever forget. What happened that night defied physics, medical expectations, and logic itself—yet Daniel walked away, shaken but alive, with a realization he would carry for the rest of his life: he had been spared for a reason.

He remembers the sky first. That evening light

that sits between gold and orange—the kind that makes everything look gentler than it really is. He had left his parents' house after Sunday dinner, the same routine every week. His mother always hugged him twice, as if the second squeeze sealed the first one in place. She didn't know that when she pulled him in that evening, she was hugging a son who would, within an hour, face the kind of violence that usually ends with families choosing caskets. Daniel later said he didn't feel afraid on the drive home. He felt something else. It was subtle at first—like the feeling you get when someone is watching you, but in a comforting way. A presence. A warmth. He couldn't name it then, but he remembered it strongly after everything happened.

He was driving his old navy-blue sedan, the one with squeaky brakes and a stubborn air conditioner that only worked when it felt like it. The radio was off, the windows were down, and he found himself humming a worship song he hadn't thought about in years. He didn't know why that song, why that moment, or why those lyrics. "You go before me... You're right beside me..." Over and over, almost involuntarily. Even later, when he replayed the night over and over in his mind, he returned to that moment. That song. That strange calm.

About ten minutes from home, the two-lane country road curved near an old cornfield. No streetlights, no shoulder, only long rows of stalks that swallowed the edges of the pavement. Daniel had driven that stretch for years, but something felt different. He eased off the gas, not out of fear but instinct. "Slow down," he would later say he heard—not out loud, but inside, like a firm whisper pressed into the space between his ribs. It came without urgency, just certainty. He didn't question it. He simply moved his foot to the brake.

He never saw the other vehicle coming. Witnesses later told investigators that a lifted truck, going over ninety miles an hour, shot across the center line after blowing a stop sign a mile up. The impact was so violent that neighbors inside nearby farmhouses felt their windows shake. One described it as "a bomb going off." The truck hit Daniel's car directly on the driver's side with such force that the entire frame folded as if made of paper. Metal screeched. Glass exploded into the night like glitter. The sedan spun, flipped twice, and then wrapped itself around a tree so completely that first responders would later say it looked like a crushed soda can.

By every scientific measure, Daniel should have died instantly.

The truck driver, tragically, did not survive. His vehicle rolled and landed upside down in a ditch. The scene was chaos—twisted metal, debris scattered across the road, steam rising from ruptured radiators. A neighbor who heard the impact rushed outside with a flashlight, expecting to find only wreckage. She didn't expect movement. But as she swept her beam across the crushed sedan, she saw—through the shattered windshield—someone shifting.

Slowly. Carefully. Almost impossibly.

Daniel does not remember the full impact, only a sudden burst of white light—bright but not painful—followed by the sensation that he was being lifted, shielded, held still. He described it later as feeling "wrapped up," as if something strong had braced around him from all sides. No tumbling, no shattering, no chaos—although chaos raged around him. He didn't feel thrown. He didn't feel crushed. He felt held. And then, as the car came to rest, he felt two firm hands press against his chest—not pushing, not restraining—just steadying. When the world stopped moving, he opened his eyes and saw only dust, smoke, and darkness. But inside, he felt the same warm presence that had whispered to him moments earlier.

The first officer on the scene approached expecting the worst. He later admitted he rehearsed what he would tell the family. When he reached the car, his flashlight froze on what remained of the driver's side. The door was crushed inward almost to the center console. The roof was peeled back. The steering wheel was bent against the seat. "No one survives this," he said into his radio, his voice heavy. But then he saw movement again—a hand, trembling but alive, rising slowly through the broken glass.

When the firefighters arrived, they didn't bother with extraction tools at first. They believed they were recovering a body. One of them prepared a sheet. Another shook his head solemnly. But then Daniel's voice—weak, hoarse, confused—broke through the air.

"I'm... I'm okay."

They froze. One firefighter actually dropped his flashlight. Another whispered, "Lord have mercy." They crowded the door, shining lights inside, trying to make sense of what they were seeing. Daniel was sitting upright—not pinned, not crushed—upright. Not a single broken bone. No major bleeding. His clothes were torn, his seatbelt frayed, and he was surrounded by the wreckage of a car that should have ended him. A paramedic looked at the car, then at Daniel, then back again, shaking his head. "This isn't possible," he said. "You should not be here."

When they lifted him from the vehicle, they discovered the impossible truth: the cabin space around Daniel had somehow remained intact despite the rest of the car collapsing. The metal around him had folded in such a way that it created a pocket—just big enough for his body to remain untouched. One firefighter pointed to the way the dashboard had crumpled in a perfect arc above Daniel's knees instead of crushing them. Another noted that a segment of the steel frame had curved outward, shielding his side like a barrier. "It bent the wrong way," one said. "It bent out instead of in. Cars don't do that."

Daniel kept trying to explain what he felt. But how do you describe something you know is real but can't prove? He told the EMT beside him, "Something kept me still. Something held me." The EMT squeezed his shoulder and nodded, not dismissing him. "I've seen a lot," he replied softly, "but I've never seen a car do… that."

At the hospital, doctors assumed internal injuries, hidden fractures, or brain trauma. They were wrong. Scan after scan came back clean. Blood work normal. Vitals steady. After several hours of observation, a young doctor entered the room carrying a clipboard and wearing an expression somewhere between disbelief and awe. "You're walking out of here," she said. "Do you understand that people don't survive crashes like that? We're trying to figure out how you did."

Daniel didn't have a scientific answer. What he had was a memory—of the whisper to slow down, of the warmth surrounding him moments before impact, of the hands he felt steadying him when the world turned upside down. He struggled at first to articulate it without sounding strange. But he eventually told them what he believed: "I wasn't alone in that car."

Survivor's guilt came early. The driver of the other vehicle was a young man, only twenty-eight, with a mother who adored him and a sister who said he made the best homemade salsa in the state. Daniel thought about him constantly. He wondered why he had been spared when another family was burying their son. The weight of that question followed him for months. Sleep was hard. Flashbacks came without warning. He would look at the twisted remains of his sedan, which had been towed to a scrapyard, and try to reconcile the image of destruction with the fact that he had walked away.

His mother reminded him gently that grief and gratitude often live in the same house. His pastor told him that being spared doesn't mean someone else was chosen to suffer—it means God wasn't finished with him yet. But Daniel wrestled anyway. He attended the funeral of the other driver, standing off to the side in a quiet corner, tears running down his face. The man's mother approached him, her steps slow but determined, and when she reached him, she did something he never expected—she embraced him. Not politely. Not reluctantly. Fully. Deeply. She held his face in her hands and said, "Don't carry this. Please. You were saved for something. Find out what it is."

Her words became a turning point. Daniel stopped asking why he lived and started asking what he was supposed to do with the life he still had. As time passed, the guilt softened—not because it disappeared, but because it was reshaped into purpose. He began to speak at youth groups about choices, faith, and the fragility of life. He visited the fire station and thanked every firefighter personally. He carried the memory of that night as both a scar and a promise.

Years later, Daniel still can't drive past that stretch of road without feeling something shift inside him. Not fear. Not trauma. Something closer to reverence. He often parks his car on the gravel shoulder, steps out, and stands quietly at the edge of the cornfield, listening to the wind move through the stalks. He remembers the whisper. He remembers the warmth. He remembers the impossible shape of the wreckage that didn't crush him.

He knows without doubt that something—someone—protected him. Not because he deserved it. Not because he was stronger or faster or lucky. But because God had a purpose for him that did not end on that road. The miracle wasn't just surviving the crash. It was everything that came after: the conversations he never would have had, the people he never would have comforted, the lessons he never would have learned.

Daniel will tell you that the defining moment of his life wasn't the crash, nor the rescue, nor the hospital discharge. It was the realization that

God's hand had been over him long before the impact. In the whisper. In the warmth. In the unseen protection that held him together when everything around him broke. He wasn't spared by accident. He was spared by grace.

Chapter Seven

Fireproof Faith

"Fire doubles in size every sixty seconds." It's a statistic most people hear once and forget, a distant danger tucked into the back of the mind—until the day it becomes personal. For the Ramirez family of Willow Creek, that number would later become a chilling echo, a reminder of how quickly life can teeter between ordinary calm and unimaginable chaos, and how God can step into the very places where fear is strongest.

The night it happened, the quiet of the small neighborhood was the kind people like to brag about living in—the kind where you can hear the gentle scrape of tree branches against windows, where porch lights flicker lazily, and where even the dogs seem to sleep more deeply. Inside the Ramirez home, the evening had played out in its usual rhythm. Dinner dishes drying by the sink. Homework scattered across the dining table. A leftover scent of pan-fried chicken still lingering faintly in the air. It was a normal Tuesday, utterly unremarkable, until the moment everything turned.

It started with a faint crackle. At first, no one noticed it. It was soft, like the faint crumpling of paper beneath something heavy. But within moments, the crackle grew into something sharper, more aggressive—an angry snapping sound coming from somewhere deep within the walls of the house. Maria Ramirez paused in the hallway, frowning, uncertain whether she had imagined it. She turned her head slightly, listening. There it was again—a sudden pop, followed by the unmistakable scent of something acrid drifting in the air.

Her heart tightened. She knew that smell. Burning plastic. Electrical wiring.

"David?" she called out, her voice catching.

Her husband emerged from the small home office at the back, rubbing his eyes after hours of computer work. "What's wrong?"

"Do you smell that?"

He took a breath, and in an instant, his expression changed. The scent was stronger now, a throb of heat pulsing behind it. Before either of them could react, a loud **BOOM** shook the house. The lights flickered once, twice, then died entirely, plunging them into a darkness that felt thick and immediate.

Maria screamed for the children. "Isaac! Lily! Come to us now!"

In the blackness, she could hear the quick patter of small feet. Isaac, nine years old, already choking on panic, grabbed his sister's hand. Lily was only five, and she whimpered as the smell intensified.

Something deep inside the house growled—like wind tearing through an open furnace—and then the orange glow appeared, faint at first, then swelling, stretching itself across the corridor, licking the walls as though claiming them. The fire had breached the attic and burst through the ceiling tiles in a violent descent.

David tried to lead them toward the front door, but smoke had already filled the living room. The air was thick, suffocating, burning their throats. Maria dropped to her knees, dragging the children down with her. "Stay low! Stay low!" she cried, repeating the words she'd once heard in a fire safety talk at Isaac's school.

Except nothing about this felt like safety. The heat pressed against her skin like an open furnace door. Flames roared behind them, spreading with monstrous speed. Another piece of ceiling fell, sending sparks scattering across the wooden floor like hot beads.

"David, the kitchen!" she shouted. "The back door!"

He tried. He pulled his shirt over his mouth and

pushed into the thick haze, but the fire had already overtaken the kitchen walls. Through the smoke, Maria could see the silhouette of flames twisting upward, blocking their only exit. They were trapped. Every door was engulfed. Every window was too hot to approach. The inferno had wrapped itself around them like a closing fist.

Isaac sobbed. "Mom, we're not going to make it!"

Maria grabbed his face gently with trembling hands. "Listen to me," she whispered, her voice firm though her body shook uncontrollably. "God is here. Do you hear me? God is here with us right now."

She didn't know where the words came

from—only that they rose within her like breath itself. And as soon as she said it, something shifted in the atmosphere. A peace she could not explain washed over her, soft and steady as warm oil poured over the head. It didn't make sense. The fire roared with a savagery that could swallow them whole, and yet her heart slowed, her breath steadied, and something inside whispered, *Stand. Don't be afraid.*

David stepped back toward them, his face streaked with sweat and soot. "Everything is blocked," he gasped. "I don't know how to get us out."

Maria reached for his hand. "We won't get out on our own."

The fire surged again, flames clawing their way

toward them. Isaac coughed, wheezing. Lily collapsed in a small heap, terrified. The smoke stung their eyes until tears poured freely. The living room ceiling groaned, bowing with the weight of destruction.

Maria closed her eyes. "Lord, we need You. We need You now."

And then—it happened.

A sudden roar of wind barreled down the hallway, but it wasn't destructive like the fire. It was cool. Strangely cool. A gust so unexpected and so forceful that it pushed the smoke upward in a swirling column, clearing the space around them. David opened his eyes wide, staring at the sudden pocket of breathable air encircling them.

"What in the world—?" he murmured, stunned.

But Maria knew. She didn't need explanation. She felt the presence—warm, strong, covering them like unseen armor. She held her children close, and though the blaze was inches away, the heat around them felt strangely muted. The wooden floor beneath them, moments away from igniting, seemed untouched. A small circle—no wider than a few feet—had become a shield, a space the fire wouldn't cross.

Outside, neighbors gathered in confusion and horror. Flames were pouring through the roof now, shooting into the night sky like flares. People screamed for someone to call 911. Some tried to approach the doors, but the fire pushed them back with scorching bursts of heat. One neighbor later recalled, "The fire was eating the house alive. There was no way anyone inside was surviving that."

Sirens wailed in the distance, getting closer. The Ramirez home burned brighter. The windows shattered one by one, sending fiery shards outward. Neighbors cried, praying aloud, pleading for the family.

Inside, Maria whispered, "God is with us. He's making a way."

And almost as if the fire itself obeyed a command, the flames to their left suddenly split—not randomly, not chaotically, but deliberately—like a curtain pulled apart from the center. A narrow path opened across the wreckage toward the hallway that led to the back door. The family had seconds. David lifted Lily into his arms. Maria held Isaac's hand so tightly her knuckles whitened.

"Go!" she yelled.

They ran. Through fire. Through heat no human body should withstand. The floorboards burned everywhere except the small strip beneath their feet. Later, firefighters would swear the burn patterns made no logical sense. The walls on each side were scorched black. The ceiling beams overhead collapsed seconds after they passed. Yet the path remained intact until the last foot crossed it.

When David kicked open the back door, a blast of fresh night air filled their lungs. They stumbled into the yard coughing, but alive. Entirely alive.

Fire crews barreled toward them, ordering them

to move farther back. One firefighter in full gear stopped short when he realized who they were. "How did you get out?" he demanded, looking from the burning doorway to the family with wide, disbelieving eyes. "The temperature in there is over a thousand degrees. Nobody survives that."

Maria tried to speak but her voice cracked. Isaac stood shaking, gripping his mother's shirt. Lily buried her face in David's shoulder.

The firefighter crouched down, gently pulling off his helmet. His face was tight with confusion, almost fear. "There's no way you walked through that."

Maria lifted her head. There were tears on her smoke-stained cheeks, but her voice was steady.

"We didn't walk alone."

The man stared at her, stunned into silence.

Neighbors rushed forward, crying, hugging, unable to understand how the family had emerged without a single burn. Not a blister, not a singe mark on their skin. Even the clothing they wore was only lightly singed at the edges.

One of the firefighters returned from inside, shaking his head. "The whole hallway is gone," he said. "The floor's collapsed. There's no structural support left. I don't understand this. I really don't."

People whispered words like unbelievable, impossible, and miracle. Some were crying openly. One teenage neighbor, still shaking, kept saying, "I saw the flames. I thought they were gone. I thought we were watching them die."

But the Ramirez family knew what they had felt inside the inferno—an overwhelming calm that made no sense, a presence that held them steady while flames raged around them, an unseen shield that refused to let the fire consume them. Maria later said it felt like standing inside a bubble of peace, a peace so thick and real it seemed to have walls.

When the flames were finally extinguished, the fire chief asked them to walk him through everything. He listened quietly, taking notes, but his expression only grew more bewildered. Eventually he closed his notepad and said, "I've been doing this for twenty-seven years. I've never heard anything like this. The fire patterns are wrong. They don't behave this way. There is no explanation."

Maria corrected him softly. "There is one."

News spread faster than the smoke had. Within hours, the story reached the local church, then the surrounding towns, and soon strangers were driving by the charred shell of the house, staring in disbelief at the place where four lives should have ended. People called it a miracle. Firefighters called it impossible. The Ramirez family called it God's grace—pure, unearned, overwhelming grace.

In the weeks that followed, something remarkable happened in the community. People who had not been to church in years asked the family to pray for them. Neighbors who barely spoke to one another began lingering on porches, retelling what they had seen, trying to make sense of the moment the flames split like a veil. Even the firefighters—tough, seasoned men who had seen everything—stood around their trucks saying, "I don't know what you believe, but something happened in there."

Isaac, once a quiet boy, began telling classmates, "God saved us." Lily drew pictures of "the angel wind," as she called it, the cool gust that had pushed the smoke away. David found himself waking up early every morning, overwhelmed with gratitude. Maria couldn't walk past a candle flame without remembering the heat that should have ended her family's story.

The burned house would eventually be torn

down, but the memory remained—a quiet plot of land holding the imprint of a miracle. And even long after the smoke cleared and the debris was gone, the story lived on in the hearts of everyone who heard it, because once you witness fire trying to take what God refuses to surrender, you never see life the same way again.

Chapter Eight

Delivered Overnight

"Nearly 21 million Americans struggle with at least one addiction, but fewer than 10% ever receive treatment. And of those who do, relapse rates often reach 40–60%, making recovery feel like an impossible climb."

This statistic stunned Daniel the first time he heard it. Not because he doubted it—but because he felt like he personally represented every failure inside that number. Every relapse. Every ruined promise. Every attempt that ended in shame. He had lived the statistics, breathed them, drowned in them. And yet, somehow, he was about to become the exception—the miracle few ever dared to hope for.

For more than a decade, Daniel's life had been shaped by cravings he could not control. It started when he was nineteen, a college sophomore who had just discovered freedom and stress in the same semester. A friend handed him a bottle one night after a brutal exam, and Daniel remembered the warmth spreading through his chest, the way laughter came easier, how the world felt softer. One drink turned into two. Two became four. And before long, alcohol was the one thing he turned to for courage, comfort, escape, and sleep.

By twenty-five, he was drinking daily. By twenty-eight, he had lost his job, totaled two cars, and destroyed the trust of everyone who cared for him. He had tried quitting—many times. He poured bottles down the sink and swore it was over. He downloaded apps for sobriety. He attended meetings when he could. Therapists encouraged him, counselors warned him, friends pleaded with him. His mother cried in the kitchen so often the sound became another part of the house. But every time Daniel tried to rise, the addiction pulled him back down, whispering that nothing in his life could change.

He had good days. He had worse days. He had days where he managed to stay sober until evening and rewarded himself with "just one," which became "just three," which inevitably led to nights he couldn't remember. His girlfriend left him after finding him passed out in the hallway of their apartment, the key still in his hand. His father stopped answering the phone after Daniel stole from him to buy more liquor. Old friends crossed the street when they saw him coming. Job applications piled up unanswered as his life shrank into rooms with closed blinds and silent phones.

He hated himself for what he was becoming. He hated the lies, the secrecy, the emptiness that grew heavier each day. He knew he was killing himself slowly, but he couldn't stop. Addiction had become his master—cold, demanding, relentless.

Then came the night everything fell apart.

It was raining, the kind that fell sideways in the wind. Daniel had been drinking heavily since late afternoon, pacing the living room with a bottle in one hand and a shaking phone in the other. He wanted to call someone. Anyone. But who still wanted to hear from him? In his fogged mind, he replayed every moment he had ruined, every bridge he had burned, every chance he had wasted. Something inside him snapped—quietly and painfully. He felt the weight of all his failures pressing down so hard he couldn't breathe.

He stumbled onto his knees beside the couch, gripping the bottle like a lifeline even as he felt it dragging him under. For the first time in his life, he said the truth out loud: "I can't do this anymore." His voice cracked. "God… if You're real… if You still care about someone like me… I need You to help me. I'm done. I can't keep living like this."

It wasn't eloquent. It wasn't organized. It

wasn't something he planned. It was raw, desperate, and broken—exactly the kind of prayer Heaven recognizes instantly.

He set the bottle on the carpet and pressed his forehead to the floor. "Please," he whispered, voice trembling. "Take this from me. I don't want it anymore."

He expected to feel ridiculous or empty or numb. Instead, something shifted in the room—subtle but unmistakable. The air felt charged, almost electric. Peace—real, quiet, overwhelming peace—flooded through him with such force that he gasped. A warmth settled in his chest, not like the artificial burn of alcohol, but a gentle, steady presence that felt alive. It washed over him, melting panic, fear, and shame like ice beneath sunlight.

He sat up, breathless, hands shaking—not from withdrawal but from something he couldn't explain. The craving that had dominated him for ten years… vanished. Completely. He stared at the bottle beside him with confusion, then shock. For the first time in his adult life, he didn't want it. Not a sip. Not a drop. Not even a taste.

He pushed it away with trembling fingers, and even the smell that usually called to him felt foreign, almost repulsive.

He didn't know what had happened, but he knew Who had done it.

That night he slept without alcohol for the first time in years. No night sweats. No dizziness. No tremors. No hallucinations. No withdrawal.

In the morning, he waited for the cravings to return, expecting the familiar pull. Nothing came. At noon he waited again. Nothing. At sunset, still nothing. By the second day, Daniel was pacing his living room with disbelief, opening cabinets and scanning shelves out of habit, only to realize the desire that once dictated his every waking moment had evaporated like mist.

He went to the mirror, eyes still tired but clearer than they had been in years, and whispered, "God… You really did it. Didn't You?"

The change was so dramatic that his mother didn't believe him when he arrived at her door sober, clean-shaven, and alert. She kept touching his face, wiping her tears, searching his eyes to see if he was lying. His father listened quietly as Daniel explained what happened, leaning back in his chair with his arms crossed tightly—until Daniel said the words, "I asked God for help, and He set me free. Instantly." His father's arms slowly dropped to his sides. He didn't speak at first. Then he nodded, almost imperceptibly, like a man witnessing something sacred.

Daniel's friends were speechless. His former pastor cried. His old counselor, who had spent countless hours trying to help him, shook his head and said softly, "Daniel... this doesn't happen. Not like this. I've never seen anything like it." Daniel simply replied, "I know. That's why they call it a miracle."

As weeks passed, the transformation reached every part of his life. He apologized to people he had hurt. He paid back debts he once ignored. He returned stolen items. He deleted contacts that fueled his addiction. He opened blinds that had been shut for years, letting sunlight flood the apartment as if declaring victory over darkness.

The cravings never returned. Not once. Doctors were puzzled. Specialists asked for details. Therapists wanted explanations. Daniel didn't have one except the truth: "God did what I couldn't do. What no one could do."

But the miracle didn't end with sobriety. Something deeper had awakened in him—a desire to rebuild, restore, and love people the way God had loved him. He joined a recovery support group, not as someone seeking help, but as someone offering hope. He prayed with others who felt too broken to rise, telling them about the night everything changed.

People listened. People cried. People believed.

Within a year, Daniel became a mentor to men battling addictions of all kinds. Some experienced slow progress. Others had setbacks. But every time he shared his story, something stirred in the room—faith rising, hearts opening, people daring to hope that what God did for Daniel, He could also do for them.

Word spread through his neighborhood, then his city. Churches invited him to speak. Families reached out for help. Even men who once avoided him in shame now sat with him, asking, "How did it happen? Can God really do that for someone like me?"

Daniel always smiled gently and answered the same way: "He did it for someone like me. And if He can reach me in my darkest place, He can reach anyone."

His family healed. His relationships restored. His purpose renewed. Daniel's life became living proof that one sincere moment of surrender can break chains a lifetime of effort cannot touch. He never forgot the years of bondage—the nights he begged for relief, the mornings he woke up sick and scared, the cycles of shame that nearly erased him. And he never forgot the moment God stepped into his living room, into his brokenness, into his weakness, and delivered him with power no human hands could replicate.

Even now, years later, when Daniel hears

someone say addiction always wins or recovery is impossible for certain people, he feels something rise in his spirit—not pride, but certainty. Because he knows what it means to be shackled. He knows what it means to be freed. And he knows that miracles aren't relics of ancient stories. They still happen. They still break chains. They still bring life where death once reigned.

He knows because he carries one inside him. Every morning. Every breath. Every step. Every year reclaimed from a past he once believed would destroy him. And although he seldom speaks about it directly, those who meet him can sense it—that quiet, radiant truth that lives behind his eyes:

When God steps into a life, even the strongest

chains fall off.

Chapter Nine

A Terminal Diagnosis That Disappeared

"More than 14 million people worldwide are told each year that their cancer is terminal. What the statistics never mention are the stories that defy prediction, the cases that leave even seasoned doctors silent, the moments when medicine reaches its limit—and something greater takes over."

The day Emma Lopez received her diagnosis, the rain had been falling in slow, steady sheets that blurred the windows of Mercy Hope Medical Center. She remembered sitting in the passenger seat of her husband's car, clutching the seatbelt so tightly that the imprint of the fabric had stayed on her palm for hours. She wasn't ready for the appointment, and she wasn't ready for the truth her doctor had hinted at a week earlier when he ordered the second round of tests—the ones he said were "to rule out anything concerning." She had felt the shift in his voice, the hesitation he tried to hide, and the way he avoided eye contact when he told her to bring someone with her to the follow-up.

Emma was only forty-six. A mother of two. A worship singer. A preschool teacher. No one expects to hear words like "inoperable" before they've even crossed the halfway point of their life.

When she and Miguel stepped into the exam room, the doctor entered slowly, as though every step carried weight. He closed the door gently behind him and held her file against his chest for a moment before sitting down, a gesture she would replay in her mind for months afterward. She had imagined many possible outcomes, but nothing prepared her for the way his lips tightened before he finally said, "Emma… I'm so sorry."

It was a mass in her pancreas, large and spread across vessels that made surgery impossible. The biopsy confirmed it was aggressive. Stage IV. The type that doesn't wait. The type that grows even when chemotherapy tries to hold it back. The kind of cancer people whisper about because its reputation is already known.

Miguel reached for her hand, but she barely felt it. The words in the room seemed to lose their meaning. The air felt thin. The fluorescent lights hummed too loudly. The doctor kept speaking—treatment options, life expectancy, support groups—but Emma heard none of it clearly. Instead, she focused on the way the clock on the wall ticked forward without mercy. Every second passing felt like a reminder of something slipping away.

When they returned to their car, she finally let herself cry. Not the quiet kind, but the kind that comes from somewhere deep, somewhere older than fear itself. Miguel pulled her into his arms, holding her so tightly that his shoulder shook beneath her tears. She later said that moment felt like the earth had opened beneath her feet and God reached out to steady her before she fell.

The news spread quickly through her church

and neighborhood. People responded the way communities often do—meals delivered to her door, text messages that said "praying," flowers placed on the porch when no one answered the bell. But prayer wasn't just a word in their community. People gathered. People believed. People pressed their faces to carpeted floors and called out to God as though Emma were their sister, their daughter, their mother.

Her pastor, Reverend Carter, organized nightly prayer at the church. The first evening, almost fifty people showed up. By the third evening, more than two hundred stood shoulder to shoulder in the sanctuary, lifting their voices in a kind of desperate faith that can only exist when human options fail. Emma attended that night, sitting in the front row with a blanket across her lap because her body had begun to lose weight rapidly.

Her friend, Maribel, remembers how thin Emma looked, her once-bright cheeks pale, her eyes covered with exhaustion. But she also remembers something else—how peace rested on her during worship as if she had stepped into a place where fear couldn't follow. When people prayed over her, she felt warmth move through her body, beginning in her chest and spreading outward. She didn't know what it meant. She didn't dare assume it meant anything at all. But she held on to the feeling long after she went home that night.

Treatment began a week later—aggressive chemotherapy paired with immunotherapy in a clinical trial. The doctors were honest from the beginning: these treatments were not meant to cure her. They were meant to give her more time. They were meant to slow things down. They were not meant to reverse anything.

The first round hit her like a storm. Nausea. Fatigue so heavy she couldn't climb the stairs without stopping. Hair loss within days. There were mornings she woke up too weak to stand, and Miguel would carry her to the living room couch, wrapping her in blankets and whispering prayers into her hair.

Their daughter, Sofia—just sixteen—began writing scripture verses on sticky notes and placing them around the house: on mirrors, on the refrigerator, on Emma's nightstand. On the darkest mornings, Emma would touch one and whisper it aloud until the anxiety faded enough to breathe.

Her son, Mateo, only ten, began sleeping on the floor next to her bed. He told a friend later, "I just needed to be close to Mom in case God decided to heal her while she was sleeping."

Through every appointment, every IV drip, every scan, her community kept praying. Members of the church split into prayer shifts—some praying at dawn, others late into the night. Messages came from churches in different states saying they had added Emma to their prayer lists. A group of women from her hometown organized a 24-hour prayer chain over a weekend, each taking a thirty-minute slot.

And then came the moment no one expected.

It was early January, several months after the diagnosis. A CT scan was scheduled to measure the tumor's progression. Emma walked into the radiology department trembling, not from fear but from fatigue. She later said she felt strangely calm, as though God had placed a hand on her back and whispered, "Go."

The radiology technician, a woman named Leah, helped her onto the table. Her voice was gentle. She had seen many patients like Emma—patients told they would not recover. She expected to see the same progression she saw every day, the slow advancement of a disease that rarely paused.

But when she looked at the images, she froze.

She clicked through them again. Then again.

She adjusted contrast, zoomed, checked previous scans. The mass was gone.

Completely.

No trace. No residual shadow. No scar tissue. No explanation.

She called the radiologist on duty, Dr. Chang, who entered the room quickly, his glasses slightly crooked as he leaned toward the screen.

"This must be an error," he muttered. "Pull up the last scan."

They displayed the one from October—clear, undeniable tumor pressing into vessels, large and unmistakable.

Then they returned to the scan taken minutes earlier.

Clear.

Dr. Chang asked for the raw data. He asked for a reprocess. He asked for confirmation markers. He asked for the machine calibration report. Then he let out a breath and said something Emma never forgot: "This does not happen. Tumors like this don't just... disappear."

He walked into the hallway where Emma sat waiting in a wheelchair.

"Mrs. Lopez," he said slowly, "your scans are... different."

She braced herself. She assumed "different" meant "worse." It usually did.

But he knelt in front of her, an unusual gesture for a physician known for his quiet professionalism. He took off his glasses, wiped them, put them back on, then looked directly at her.

"There's no tumor," he said. "None. I don't have a medical explanation."

Emma's breath caught. Miguel, who had stepped out to get coffee, returned just in time to see her crying in a way he hadn't seen since the diagnosis—deep, shaking, disbelieving sobs, but this time mixed with overwhelming joy.

That night, the prayer meeting at the church overflowed. People stood in aisles, in the lobby, outside under the cold air with hands lifted to the sky. Reverend Carter wept openly at the pulpit. "We asked," he said, "and Heaven answered."

Reporters later tried to interview Dr. Chang, but he refused to take credit or make assumptions. The only statement he gave was to the hospital board: "I am trained to trust science, but this event lies beyond it."

Her oncologist, Dr. Reyes, repeated her review of the entire case three times. She compared biopsy pathology reports, treatment schedules, blood work, imaging archives. She even called two colleagues in New York for outside opinions. Every specialist said the same thing: "We have never seen a reversal like this."

The mass had not shrunk.

It had vanished.

As though it had never existed.

Emma returned to the church the following

Sunday, still thin, still recovering from the harsh months behind her, but standing on her own for the first time in weeks. When she stepped onto the stage to give her testimony, the room fell silent. Her voice trembled as she began to speak about God's presence during the diagnosis, His comfort on nights when she couldn't sleep, His strength when she was too weak to stand, and His healing power that arrived without warning, without explanation, and without hesitation.

People listened, some crying quietly, others gripping the edge of their seats, as she described the moment she heard Dr. Chang say the words she never thought she would hear. She described the look on her husband's face, the way her daughter fell to her knees in the parking lot, the way her son said, "I knew God wasn't finished with you."

Even months later, the medical team continued to bring up her case during rounds and department meetings. New residents learned about her chart as an example of outcomes medicine could not account for. Some used the word "spontaneous remission," but even that didn't fit. There was no gradual improvement. No slow shrinkage. No partial response. One scan showed a large tumor. The next showed nothing.

Emma would say at the end of every interview, "It wasn't remission. God healed me."

And every time she said it, she felt the same warmth she had felt that night in the sanctuary when hundreds prayed for her—something unexplainable, something holy, something that reminded her that miracles still happened in places where hope runs thin, and that sometimes God does the impossible simply because His children ask.

Chapter Ten

"I Forgave—and God Healed Me"

"Holding onto anger is like drinking poison and expecting the other person to die."

The quote has been repeated in sermons, counseling rooms, and quiet conversations between friends for years, yet few truly understand the depths of its truth until their own hearts begin to feel the weight of bitterness. Maya didn't understand it either—not until her body began to break down under the pressure of wounds she had sworn she'd never revisit. Unforgiveness, she would later say, is a silent sickness. It doesn't announce itself like a fever or a broken bone. It hides beneath habits, memories, and the strong façade of someone who insists they are "fine." But what lives in the heart eventually speaks through the body, and Maya's body had been speaking for years.

She grew up in a small Midwestern town where church bells rang every Sunday morning and everyone knew each other's business by Monday afternoon. Her childhood was simple—bike rides after school, summers at the local lake, and a mother who prayed over her each morning before she ran out the door. But beneath all the warmth of that small-town life, one shadow lingered: her father. His anger was unpredictable, loud, and sharp. Some days he was simply distant, other days he erupted with words that cut as deeply as any blade. For years, she tried to win his affection—straight A's, perfect behavior, making herself small so that she wouldn't trigger his wrath. None of it worked. She left home at eighteen with a scholarship letter in one hand and a silent vow in her heart: *I will never forgive him. I will never speak to him again.*

For a while, freedom felt real. College brought newness—new friends, new classes, new dreams. But every time she passed a family laughing together on the campus lawn, something inside her tightened. She told herself it was nothing. She told herself forgiveness wasn't necessary. After all, she was doing fine. She had escaped. The past was behind her.

But the past has a way of finding a home in the body.

By her late twenties, she began experiencing sharp, unexplainable pain in her chest. Doctors tested her heart, her lungs, her blood—everything appeared normal. There were no blockages, no infections, no evidence of disease. The pain grew worse during stressful seasons and disappeared during moments of distraction. It became a cycle she couldn't understand. Then came the insomnia, migraines that left her curled on the bathroom floor, anxiety that tightened around her like a fist. At first, she attributed it to burnout. Her job as an elementary school teacher had grown demanding, and she told herself she simply needed rest.

Rest didn't help.

She tried counseling, nutrition changes, exercise, meditation apps—nothing touched the underlying ache. Her body was screaming, but she didn't yet know the language it was speaking.

One Sunday morning, after months of sleepless nights and escalating pain, she found herself sitting alone in a pew at a little church near her apartment. She hadn't been to church since college, but something had drawn her there—not desire, not curiosity, but desperation. The worship team began to sing softly, and she felt an odd discomfort rise in her chest, the same pain she had been battling for years. She pushed her hand against her sternum as if she could silence it. Tears pricked her eyes, but she forced them back.

Then the pastor stepped to the pulpit. He opened his Bible and said five words she never expected to hear: *"Today we're talking about forgiveness."*

She almost walked out. The word itself felt like an arrow to the heart. She sank deeper into the pew, arms crossed tightly, ready to ignore everything. But the pastor continued.

He spoke about Jesus healing the paralyzed man lowered from the roof. Not about the mat, not about the crowd, not about the miracle of walking—but the moment before the miracle. *"Your sins are forgiven."* The pastor emphasized that Jesus addressed the man's heart before He touched his body. "Sometimes," he said, "the healing we crave cannot come until the bitterness we carry is released."

His words caught her off guard. It felt like someone had peeled back a layer of her soul she had long buried. She tried to shake it off. Dozens of people packed the room—surely this message wasn't for her. But the pastor continued speaking as if looking straight into her.

"Unforgiveness," he said quietly, "is not a prison for the person who hurt you. It is a prison for the one who holds the key."

Her chest tightened again—this time not from the familiar physical pain, but from something deeper. She bowed her head, trying to stop the tears threatening to rise. For the first time in years, she felt the Holy Spirit pressing gently, insistently, on the door of a room she had locked away since childhood.

When the service ended, she lingered behind.

Her legs trembled as she approached the front. She didn't know why she was walking. She didn't want to talk to anyone. She just wanted the pain—emotional and physical—to stop. The pastor noticed her and stepped toward her slowly, as if approaching a wounded animal.

"What's hurting you?" he asked softly.

For a moment, she couldn't speak. Her throat tightened. When she finally found her voice, it cracked open like a broken dam. She told him everything—her father's anger, the years of fear, the vow she had made to herself. She admitted the cold truth she had never said aloud: "I hate him. And I hate that I hate him."

The pastor listened without a single interruption. When she finished, he nodded gently. "That hatred has kept you alive, hasn't it?" he said. She blinked, startled. She had never thought of it that way. But it was true. The hatred had once been a shield, a form of survival.

"But now," he continued, "it's keeping you from living."

She closed her eyes. She knew he was right. She also knew what he was about to say, and every cell in her body recoiled.

"You need to forgive him."

She shook her head immediately. "I can't," she whispered. "I don't know how."

"Forgiveness," he said, "is not a feeling. It's a decision. God can do the healing, but you must open the door."

Those words haunted her for days. Every night she lay in bed staring at the ceiling, the same four words circling her mind: *I need to forgive him.* She argued with herself, she cried, she resisted, she pushed it away. Why should she forgive someone who never apologized? Who never admitted the pain he caused? Why should she do the work when he had done the damage?

Because the damage was no longer his. It was hers.

One evening, after a particularly painful migraine, she fell to her knees in the middle of her living room. The floor felt cold beneath her palms. Her breath trembled. For the first time in her life, she didn't have the strength to fight the conviction inside her. She whispered into the emptiness around her, "God, help me forgive him. I don't know how to do this on my own."

She expected silence. Instead, something gentle washed over her—something warm, steady, indescribably peaceful. It was as if God Himself wrapped His presence around her, soft as a blanket but strong as an anchor. She felt no condemnation, no pressure, only an invitation.

Her tears fell freely. She didn't have flowery words or eloquent prayer. She choked out the simplest, hardest sentence she had ever spoken: "I forgive him."

The moment the words left her lips, something happened—something she could never fully explain. The tension in her chest, the pain that had shadowed her for years, suddenly released. It didn't fade gradually or lessen over time; it lifted instantly. It was as if someone had cut a rope she didn't know had been tied around her heart.

She gasped and pressed her hand against her chest in disbelief. The pain was gone. Completely gone. She sat on the floor sobbing, overwhelmed. She didn't hear a voice, didn't see a vision, but she felt something unmistakable: freedom.

The next morning, she expected the pain to return. But it didn't. The migraine that had tormented her for weeks vanished. Her breathing felt lighter. Her shoulders relaxed in a way she hadn't experienced since childhood. When she went back to the doctor a week later, every test came back clear. Her physician, puzzled, asked what changed.

"I forgave," she whispered.

The doctor didn't understand. But she did.

Forgiveness hadn't excused what her father did. It hadn't erased the wounds or rewritten her past. It hadn't turned him into someone safe or trustworthy. But it had released her from bondage. It had lifted the weight that had been crushing her from the inside. It had healed what doctors couldn't diagnose and counselors couldn't touch. It had opened a door that had been locked for decades, allowing the grace of God to pour into every cracked and broken place.

Weeks later, she wrote her father a letter—not to reconcile, not to pretend nothing happened, but to release him. She didn't mail it. She didn't need to. The forgiveness was already complete.

Over time, the emotional healing followed the physical. Her nightmares faded. Her anxiety loosened its grip. She began sleeping through the night. Prayer became easier, worship felt lighter. She found herself smiling more, laughing more, living more. Her friends noticed. Her coworkers noticed. But most importantly, she noticed.

God had not simply healed her body. He had healed her heart. And in doing so, He restored the years she thought trauma had stolen. She often said the miracle wasn't that her father changed—it was that she did. Through an act she once believed impossible, she discovered something extraordinary: forgiveness is the doorway to freedom, and freedom is God's greatest gift to the wounded.

And whenever she tells her story today, she speaks with a quiet confidence that only someone who has walked through darkness can carry. She says that forgiveness didn't erase the past but redeemed it. It didn't justify the pain but released its chains. It didn't change the person who hurt her but transformed the person she became.

Sometimes, she still hears the pastor's words echoing in her memory: *God can do the healing, but you must open the door.* And she knows now, with complete certainty, that opening that door was the miracle God had been waiting to give her all along.

Chapter Eleven

The Missing Child Found Through Prayer

"For he shall give His angels charge over you, to keep you in all your ways." — Psalm 91:11

It was the kind of spring morning that usually carried no warnings—mild sunlight, a soft breeze, birdsong drifting lazily above the treetops. But at 9:17 a.m., when eight-year-old Emily Carter slipped out the back door of her family's farmhouse in rural Tennessee, the peace of the day was shattered in ways no one could have imagined. She was supposed to be playing in the yard while her mother folded laundry. She often wandered around the property but never far—never without telling someone where she was going.

When her mother, Megan, stepped outside ten minutes later and called her name, she expected the familiar burst of footsteps racing toward her. Instead, the wind carried her voice into an empty yard. She called again—louder this time. There was still no reply. Her hands began to tremble as she walked quickly to the edge of the property where the grass dipped toward a line of woods. "Emily!" she shouted, her voice cracking in ways she couldn't control.

Still nothing.

Panic pulsed through her chest. She tried to steady her breath, reminding herself that children wander all the time. She told herself Emily had probably followed a stray kitten again or gotten distracted by wildflowers. But the fear pressing into her ribs didn't feel ordinary. It felt like something invisible had shifted. Something she couldn't name.

By 10:02 a.m., Megan had called her husband, Michael, who was working construction two towns over. By 10:19, he was racing down the gravel driveway. By 10:23, they were both in the woods shouting their daughter's name until their voices went raw, their legs burning from the uneven terrain. Emily's pink jacket, the one she'd been wearing that morning, was not lying discarded near the creek. Her butterfly hair clip was not caught in the brambles. The woods gave no clues, no signs, no comfort.

By 11:07 a.m., they had called 911.

The sheriff's department arrived with volunteers, neighbors, and an emergency search team. A helicopter circled overhead by noon. Someone brought scent dogs. Someone else pulled up a map of the terrain on a tablet. Radios crackled with voices calling out zones, grids, perimeters. Every minute that passed without finding the girl made the adults' shoulders sag a little more. What began as concern hardened into dread.

There were old wells on properties farther out. Abandoned barns. A river that swelled in spring. Coyotes in the deeper parts of the forest. The sheriff tried not to say any of this to the Carters, but the fear in his eyes gave him away. He had seen this before. Missing children. Time slipping too fast. Hope thinning.

Megan sank onto a fallen log as if her legs couldn't hold her anymore. She clutched Emily's small denim jacket against her chest. "God, please," she whispered, choking on the words. "Please don't take her from me."

Michael kept pacing, his hands shaking uncontrollably. He hadn't prayed in years—not since losing his brother in a car accident. But grief has a way of breaking open doors long shut, and as he stared into the sky, all he could say was, "If You're real, help us. Help her."

Searchers spread out in every direction. Hours passed. Sunlight thinned. No one found anything.

Then something changed.

Around 3:33 p.m., Megan was standing alone

near the old oak tree at the edge of their property when she felt something she couldn't explain—an overwhelming stillness that settled over her like warm air. It was sudden, unmistakable. The noise from the searchers faded into a distant hum. She later said it felt as though the world had paused. And then she heard something—not with her ears, but deep inside, a voice that wasn't her own. Three quiet words:

"Go to the field."

She blinked hard, unsure if stress had finally fractured her mind. But the impression didn't leave. It grew stronger. Insistent. She clutched her chest, breathing deeply, trying to make sense of it. The "field" wasn't a place they'd searched. It was an overgrown meadow two miles from the property line, past a stretch of forest that Emily didn't know how to reach.

Megan ran to the sheriff. "I need to go to the field," she said breathlessly.

"We've searched that area," he said gently. "There's nothing there. Ma'am, you're exhausted. Let's—"

"You haven't searched the field," she snapped back, surprising herself. "Not that one. The old Peterson field behind the ridge."

The sheriff frowned. He knew the one—abandoned for decades, barely accessible. It wasn't even on their search plan. "There's no reason she would go that far."

"I just know," she whispered, tears spilling. "Please."

He stared at her for a long moment. Something in her face—desperation or conviction, he didn't know—made him radio two deputies. "Let's check it," he said reluctantly. "Just to be thorough."

Megan insisted on going, though she was trembling. Michael followed. They climbed into the sheriff's vehicle and sped down the old dirt road that led near the ridge. They parked half a mile out and hiked the rest. The forest was dense, branches scratching at their arms as they pushed through. Leaves crushed under their shoes in the hush of late afternoon. Megan's heart pounded with every step, fear and strange certainty battling inside her.

When they reached the ridge, Megan felt it again—a pulse in her chest, as though her spirit recognized the place. She ran downhill before anyone else, stumbling over rocks, scraping her palms, not feeling the pain. The field came into view—a sea of tall grass bending slightly in the wind.

Then she heard it.

A sound so faint she wasn't sure it was real. A whimper. A cry. The kind a child makes when she's run out of strength.

"Emily?" Megan screamed, her voice cracking.

A second whimper. Louder. To the left.

Megan tore through the grass, her legs burning, her lungs on fire. Michael sprinted beside her, calling his daughter's name again and again. The deputies followed behind, disbelief already spreading across their faces.

And there—in a patch of flattened grass, dirt smudged on her cheeks, a bruise on her forehead, her tiny hands scraped and shaking—was Emily Carter.

She was curled up, exhausted, dehydrated, frightened, but alive.

Megan collapsed onto her knees, sobbing uncontrollably as she pulled her daughter into her arms. Emily cried too, burying her face in her mother's shirt. Michael knelt beside them, his hands trembling as he cupped Emily's head, whispering, "Thank You, God… thank You…"

Emily explained through tears that she had followed a stray puppy she'd seen near the woods. She thought it needed help. She never caught it but kept walking deeper until she didn't recognize anything. She fell down the ridge. She hit her head. She tried calling for help, but no one heard her. She sat in the field for hours, praying for someone to find her.

"I asked God to tell you where I was," she whispered to her mother.

Megan sobbed harder.

The deputies radioed in the news, voices shaky with relief. The sheriff arrived minutes later, wiping his eyes as he stared at the girl who should never have been found that far out. The helicopter circled overhead and then peeled away. Search teams were told to stand down. The news spread through the community in seconds. People gasped, cheered, cried, and clung to each other in disbelief.

The sheriff later told reporters he had no explanation for how Megan knew exactly where to go. The field wasn't mapped as a search zone. It was miles away from where anyone expected a child to wander. The terrain between the property and the ridge was rugged. Emily had no water, no sense of direction, no way to climb back toward home. Even the deputies admitted the location made no logical sense.

But Megan and Michael knew.

They knew the instant they saw their daughter lying in that grass.

They knew the moment Megan felt that stillness at the oak tree.

They knew the moment Emily whispered, "I asked God to tell you."

Word spread across the region. A story like this grows its own wings, carried from front porches to church pews, from schools to break rooms and grocery aisles. People repeated it with the awe of those trying to understand something beyond human reasoning. Families prayed together. Pastors shared the testimony on Sunday mornings. The sheriff's office received letters from strangers amazed by what had happened.

Weeks later, when a local news station interviewed the Carters, Megan spoke softly but clearly. "People can explain it however they want. They can say it was instinct or coincidence or desperation. But I know what I heard. God told me where my daughter was."

Michael nodded beside her, his hand wrapped

securely around hers. "We didn't deserve this miracle," he said, his voice thick with gratitude. "But God gave it anyway."

Emily sat between them, healthy, smiling shyly, swinging her legs off the chair. She held her mother's hand with a quiet confidence, as though she too had seen something she couldn't fully describe—something holy, something powerful, something that would shape her understanding of God for the rest of her life.

The sheriff, interviewed separately, shook his head slowly and said, "I've been doing this job for over twenty-five years. I've seen cases that didn't end well. Cases you never forget. But this family… what happened out there… it wasn't normal. I don't pretend to understand it. I just know that child shouldn't have been found alive. Not where she was. Not after that long. Something led that mother straight to her."

The reporter asked him if he believed it was divine intervention.

The sheriff looked down for a moment, then answered, "I believe something bigger than us was at work that day."

In the months that followed, Megan sometimes woke in the night and replayed that moment at the oak tree—the sudden stillness, the whisper she didn't hear with her ears but with her soul. She would lie awake marveling that God had spoken so clearly, so personally, so powerfully. Emily would occasionally crawl into bed beside her. She'd rest her head on her mother's shoulder and say, "God helped us, didn't He?"

And Megan would whisper back, "Yes, baby. He did."

The field where Emily was found became a place of quiet reverence for the Carters, a spot where heaven had touched earth in a way that could never be forgotten. Sometimes, Michael would mow a small path around the ridge and stand there alone, tears forming as he remembered the terror of that day and the miracle that followed. Sometimes he would pray—really pray—for the first time in years.

Emily grew older, but the memory stayed vivid. Her rescue became part of her identity, a reminder that she was never alone, that God watched over her even when she was afraid. And her parents never stopped telling the story—not for attention, not for sympathy, but so people would know that God still speaks, still guides, still rescues, still works miracles in the world today.

The sheriff kept a copy of the case file in his desk drawer, labeled not under "missing child" but under a word he rarely used. A word he never used lightly.

Miracle.

Chapter Twelve

A Whisper in the Storm

"Most people never hear God because they're too busy listening for something loud." — Dallas Willard

The storm came without warning—no dark line across the horizon, no shift in the pressure that old fishermen always claim they can feel in their bones. The weather report had been confident: mild winds, gentle swells, calm seas throughout the late afternoon. Nothing unusual for early June. Nothing that would send Daniel Reyes back to shore. He had made this journey a thousand times, following the same familiar route out of the bay, cutting across the deep-blue water that always reminded him of his father's stories about faith, risk, and the sea.

Daniel had been fishing since he was five years old. Some of his earliest memories were of watching his father pull in nets with hands roughened by salt and sun. Fishing was in his blood, a calling as old as his family name, and the ocean was the closest he ever felt to God. But as he pushed his small boat into deeper waters that afternoon, he felt something he couldn't explain—an unexpected chill that slid down the back of his neck, even though the air was warm. Almost as if someone had gently brushed their fingers against his skin. Soft. Quick. Thoughtful.

He ignored it. Fishermen learned to ignore strange feelings. If they reacted to every flicker of intuition, they'd never leave the shore.

For hours the water remained steady, the kind of smooth that made casting lines feel almost leisurely. Daniel caught enough mackerel and redfish to fill half the cooler. Not a bad day, he thought. Not the best either. But the sea owed him nothing, and he had never been one to push his luck.

It wasn't until the sun began dipping into the horizon that he noticed the first odd change—birds. Gulls that normally soared and hovered above his boat suddenly abandoned the air, flying hard and fast toward shore as if chased by something unseen. Then the surface of the water rippled with a strange, unnatural shiver, like a warning whispered through the waves.

Daniel stood up, narrowing his eyes at the open

water. He saw nothing. No storm clouds. No signs of danger. The air was still. Yet inside him something tightened, something old—instinct, perhaps. Or something deeper. He reached for the radio to call in early, but the moment he pressed the button, all he heard was static.

He turned the dial. Static.
 Checked the backup radio. Static.

It was then that the wind arrived—sudden, violent, slamming into his boat with enough force to jolt it sideways. The metal hull groaned. Daniel grabbed the railing to keep from stumbling. Another gust hit, stronger, almost angry. The calm ocean transformed in seconds into a writhing field of whitecaps.

The sky darkened so quickly it felt unnatural, as

if someone had flipped a switch. A massive wall of clouds surged across the horizon, layered and thick, swallowing the last traces of daylight. Thunder cracked open the sky. Lightning cut jagged paths through the darkness, each strike closer than the last.

What had been a peaceful evening was now something fierce and unpredictable.

Daniel's breathing quickened. His hands trembled—not from fear, he told himself, but from adrenaline. Yet deep inside, he felt something he hadn't felt since he was twelve years old, the night a storm pulled his father's boat under. The sea had taken his father before dawn broke. They found the empty boat days later, battered, half-sunk, nets tangled like abandoned memories.

And now the ocean looked exactly like it had that night—wild, consuming, merciless.

"Not again," Daniel whispered to himself, gripping the wheel. "Not like this."

He started the engine. The boat roared to life—then sputtered. Choked. Died.

He tried again.

And again.

Nothing.

Rain fell hard, sheets of it slamming against him with a stinging force. It blurred the water, the horizon, everything. Daniel turned his back against the wind, shielding his eyes. Water seeped into his boots, his clothes, chilling him to the bone.

For the first time in years, he felt the cold edge

of real fear.

Not the kind that brushed against your mind.

The kind that settled deep into your chest, heavy and suffocating.

Lightning illuminated the world for a second—just long enough for him to see the waves swelling taller, as if the sea had grown teeth. One wave hit the side of the boat with a violent slap, sending icy water over the deck. Daniel used all his strength to steady himself, every muscle tense, his heart pounding so loud he could hear it over the storm.

He had only one thought:

I might not make it home.

The storm screamed around him, the wind howling like a living thing. Daniel shouted into the roar, hoping the radio might miraculously pick up his voice. "Mayday! Mayday! This is vessel Seastar—engine failure—caught in sudden storm—"

Nothing. Only static.

His hands shook as they clutched the wheel. The rain stung his eyes. He could barely see an arm's length in front of him. The world had shrunk into a circle of darkness and chaos. There was no shore. No direction. No hope. Just noise. Just fear. Just the storm.

Then—

In the middle of the chaos—

In the roar of wind and water—

Something impossible happened.

A whisper.

So soft it felt like it came from inside him.

So gentle it seemed to rise only when everything else fell silent.

Turn left, Daniel.

He froze.

He had not imagined it.

He knew he had not imagined it.

It wasn't his father's voice.

Not his mother's.

Not his own.

It was calm, steady, warm—like someone speaking just behind his shoulder, close enough to touch.

He turned his head. No one was there.

He swallowed hard, confusion mixing with terror.

He wanted to ignore it. He wanted to rely on reason. But reason had abandoned him the moment the storm swallowed the sky.

The whisper came again.

Softer this time.

More urgent.

Turn left.

Daniel gripped the wheel tighter, his throat tight with emotion. "God... is that You?"

The wind howled, but the whisper remained.

Gentle. Patient.

Like the kind of guidance given to a child taking their first steps.

He didn't know why, but he obeyed.

He turned the wheel left.

The boat resisted, the storm pushing hard

against the shift, but Daniel forced it through.

Then another whisper.

Forward.

The boat lurched. A wave crashed against the hull. Daniel held on so tightly that his knuckles turned white. He ignored everything but the whisper—the only sound in the world that didn't want to destroy him.

Minutes passed, each one feeling like an hour.

The storm raged on, but something was different.

The waves were still enormous, but they no longer slammed against the boat with the same fury. The wind remained fierce, but it wasn't pushing him backward anymore.

The whisper continued, always simple:

Left. Right. Straight. Hold on.

Daniel did exactly as it said.

He didn't question.

He didn't doubt.

Every fiber in him understood that this was not instinct.

Not imagination.

It was guidance.

It was protection.

It was grace.

Then—

Just as suddenly as it had begun—

The storm broke.

The rain softened.

The thunder drifted away.

The clouds opened, revealing a faint glimmer

of moonlight cutting through the darkness. The waves calmed enough for the boat to rock gently instead of violently. Daniel let out a breath he didn't realize he had been holding.

He looked around, dazed, exhausted, soaked to the bone. And then he saw it.

Light.
 A single light.
 Not bright—but steady.

He blinked, wiping rain and tears from his face. It was a buoy.
 One he recognized.
 A channel marker he had passed every week for the past fifteen years.

He was less than a mile from shore.
 The storm had carried him farther than he ever

imagined—but the whisper had guided him back into familiar waters, threading him through darkness like an unseen hand.

Daniel dropped to his knees on the deck, breath shaking, heart full. He whispered words he hadn't spoken aloud in years. "Thank You. Thank You, Lord. Thank You for not leaving me."

The truth settled deep into his spirit as the boat drifted toward safety:

He had been alone in the storm, but he had not been abandoned.

He had been surrounded by chaos, but God had spoken through the whisper.

He had been lost, but grace had found him.

Many people asked him later how he survived

that storm—how he kept his boat steady, how he found his way back when visibility was gone and the radio wasn't working. Some assumed he had years of experience. Others chalked it up to luck.

Daniel knew better.

There was no debate in his heart.

He had not saved himself.

He had not found his way out.

Something greater had stepped into the storm with him.

And sometimes, God doesn't shout.

He doesn't split the sky.

He doesn't send thunder or flames.

Sometimes, He simply whispers.

And that whisper is enough to pull a soul from

the edge of death back into life.

Chapter Thirteen

When God Sends the Right Person at the Right Time

"Some miracles do not arrive with lightning and thunder. Sometimes they come quietly, disguised as ordinary people who appear for only a moment—but leave behind a lifetime of proof that God was paying attention."

There are stories that circle through communities for decades, told in whispers at family dinners and repeated in testimonies long after the details fade. Stories so strange, so perfectly timed, so impossibly precise that even skeptics feel a shiver run through them when they hear them. Stories like this one—because every once in a while, heaven seems to send someone into our world for only a heartbeat, just long enough to rewrite the ending that seemed already sealed.

It was late November, the kind of evening that settles heavily over a town and swallows the last bit of daylight before most people have finished their routines. The air was dry and sharp, and a chilled wind drifted across the highway, nudging loose leaves across the asphalt like restless thoughts. Lauren had been on the road for hours, driving home from her mother's house with the kind of exhaustion that wraps itself around the bones. She knew she should have left earlier, but goodbyes always ran long—especially now that her mother's health was declining. She wanted to stay, but she also needed to get back to her children waiting at home. The road stretched ahead in long shadows, illuminated only by her headlights.

The highway was quiet, almost eerily so. Traffic usually pulsed through that stretch, even at night, but on this evening she seemed to be the only one traveling east. Her phone battery had died miles ago, and she'd forgotten her charger on her mother's kitchen table. She told herself it was fine—she'd driven this road enough times to know every bend and every mile marker. But she wished she had the comfort of hearing her children's voices before they went to bed.

Somewhere around mile marker 114, just as the road dipped into a narrow stretch bordered by a ditch on one side and a steep embankment on the other, she heard a grinding noise under her car. At first it was faint, barely noticeable, but it grew quickly—an urgent, metallic groan that rattled beneath her feet. She eased off the gas and tried to pull over, but the steering wheel jerked violently to one side. The tire blew out with a sound like a shotgun blast. The car spun, skidding across the lane, and Lauren fought the wheel with every ounce of strength she had. It finally came to rest near the edge of the ditch, nose angled downward, the front tire shredded and rubber scattered across the pavement.

She sat there gripping the wheel, her heart hammering. The silence that followed was suffocating. No cars passed. No lights appeared on the horizon. The cold air seeped in through the cracked window, brushing against her face like an unwelcome reminder of how alone she truly was.

She tried her phone again, pressing the power button even though she knew better. Nothing. Her nearest family was hours away. The closest service station was more than fifteen miles behind her. She considered walking, but the darkness around her made the world feel enormous and impossibly distant. There were no houses nearby. No buildings. Just miles of highway swallowed by night.

She whispered a prayer—not a polished, well-crafted prayer, but the kind that spills out when everything else has run dry. "God, please… I don't know what to do. I need help."

The wind answered with a long, low sigh across the open fields. Lauren pulled her coat tighter and stepped out of the car. The road stretched empty in both directions, the only sound the soft creaking of her cooling engine. Part of her wondered how long it would take for another driver to pass. An hour? Two? She couldn't wait that long. Her children were expecting her. Her mother would worry if she didn't check in. And standing on the side of a deserted highway felt like standing on the edge of a cliff.

She walked around the car, trying to assess the damage. The tire was gone—completely destroyed. The rim was bent. She didn't have a spare; she'd meant to replace it months ago but life kept pushing it down the list. A cold knot formed in her chest. She leaned her hands on the hood and let the reality settle in. There was no solution she could reach on her own. Not tonight.

A few minutes passed, though it felt like longer. She kept glancing up and down the road, hoping to see headlights. Nothing came. The stillness pressed in around her until she felt something inside her begin to break. It wasn't fear—not exactly. It was the weight of being helpless, the kind of helplessness that comes when every plan, every backup, every sense of control slips through your fingers. She whispered again, softer this time. "Please, God. Send someone."

She meant it as a small prayer, barely more than a breath. She didn't expect anything to happen. But sometimes God listens in ways we do not see coming.

She had just stepped back toward her driver's

door when she noticed movement in her rearview mirror. Faint headlights crested the hill behind her, two soft beams growing brighter. She stood still, watching them approach, unsure whether to be relieved or afraid. The car slowed as it neared, then stopped a few yards behind her. The driver's door opened with a creak she could hear even over the wind.

A man stepped out. Middle-aged, tall, wearing a dark coat and a knit cap pulled low over his ears. His boots made soft thuds as he walked toward her, but something about his posture was calm, steady—like he belonged in the moment in a way she didn't. She felt a flicker of peace move through her, unexpected and warm.

"Ma'am, are you okay?" he asked, his voice gentle.

Lauren hesitated. She had been warned her whole life about strangers on the road, but something in his expression disarmed her. There was a kindness in his eyes, not intrusive or forceful—just present.

"My tire blew out," she said. "My phone is dead. I can't call for help."

He nodded slowly, as if this was exactly the situation he had expected to find. "Let's have a look."

He knelt beside the damaged tire, brushing his hand over the shredded rubber. "You're not driving anywhere on this. But don't worry—I'll take care of it."

She blinked. She hadn't even seen his car clearly yet. "You have a spare?"

"I've got something better," he replied with a small smile. "I've done roadside assistance for years. You'd be surprised how often people end up stranded right when they need someone most."

He went back to his truck and returned with tools she couldn't even name. A portable jack, an air compressor, something that looked like a heavy-duty wrench, and a spare he said would fit just well enough to get her to the next service station. She didn't know how he knew her model or what she needed, but he spoke with the quiet confidence of someone who had solved this problem a hundred times.

He worked efficiently, without hesitation. The cold didn't seem to bother him. Lauren watched him, realizing she didn't even know his name.

She felt the urge to ask where he was headed, why he had been driving down such a lonely stretch at that hour, but she didn't want to break the strange, peaceful concentration he worked with. It felt like interrupting something sacred.

Within twenty minutes, he stood and wiped his hands on a cloth he pulled from his coat pocket. "All set." He lowered the car gently from the jack and tested the tire. "This will hold. Drive carefully to the service station about eleven miles up the road. They'll replace it properly."

Lauren exhaled as if she'd been holding her breath the entire night. "I don't know how to thank you."

"You already did," he said simply, as though the act of helping her was all the thanks he needed.

She stepped forward slightly. "Can I at least know your name?"

He smiled again, softer this time. "Maybe another day." He turned back toward his truck.

"Wait," she called after him. "Please—can I give you something? Anything?"

He paused before opening his door. "No need. Just get home safe."

She nodded, swallowing the lump in her throat. "I will."

He gave her a small wave, climbed into his truck, and pulled away from the shoulder. She expected to see his headlights disappearing in the distance, but the moment he turned the corner, the road ahead went dark as if he'd vanished into the night. She waited a few seconds, then slid into her own car and started the engine. It purred to life, smooth and steady.

As she pulled onto the highway, she kept glancing at her mirror, expecting to see the man's truck behind her. But the road was empty again, stretching in both directions without a single sign of another vehicle. It was as though he had arrived from nowhere and returned just as quietly.

When she finally made it home—nearly an hour later than expected—her children ran to her, clinging to her coat and asking why she was late. She held them closer than usual, feeling the weight of what could have happened. As she tucked them into bed, the stranger's face kept appearing in her mind: calm, reassuring, almost impossibly peaceful. She wondered who he had been, where he had come from, and why he had stopped for her on an otherwise empty road.

But most of all, she wondered why his presence had felt so familiar, as though she had been waiting for him without even knowing it.

In the days that followed, she mentioned the experience to friends and neighbors. Some nodded knowingly, saying it sounded like the kind of good Samaritan story that restores your faith in the world. Others suggested it was dangerous to trust a stranger on the roadside. But Lauren felt none of that. She knew, deep in her spirit, that something had happened that night—something she couldn't explain and didn't need to.

She returned to the location days later, hoping

to recognize his truck or see another sign of him. But the highway was just a highway, ordinary and unchanged. She asked attendants at the service station if they knew a man who matched the description—a roadside technician, perhaps, or a local volunteer. No one did.

It was as if he never existed at all.

That realization didn't frighten her. It humbled her. Because she remembered something her grandmother used to say: "God sends the right people at the right time. Sometimes they stay. Sometimes they only visit once. But they always leave you changed."

That night on the side of the road had changed her. She prayed differently now, not out of desperation but out of gratitude. She lived with a new awareness that she was not unseen or unheard. And whenever she told her story—which she eventually did, often—she always said the same thing:

"I wasn't alone that night. God sent someone. I still don't know who he was. But God does. And that's the miracle."

She never concluded the story with certainty, because the beauty of the moment lay in its mystery. The stranger's arrival felt too perfectly timed, too precisely equipped, too strangely peaceful to be coincidence. And whether he was an angel, a messenger, or simply a man led by God's quiet whisper, his presence was proof that help can arrive in the exact second it's needed—without warning, without explanation, and without ever returning again.

And that is how God often works, slipping into the cracks of the impossible, sending the right person at the right time, guiding events so delicately and precisely that only in hindsight do we realize the miracle that unfolded in front of us.

Chapter Fourteen

Provision in the Final Hour

"God is never late. He is never early. He arrives at the exact moment when human strength ends and divine help begins." It's a phrase people repeat in church halls and prayer circles, but the weight of that truth isn't fully understood until a person stands at the edge—when rent is due, the fridge is empty, the bills are stacked high on the kitchen table, and there is nothing left to do but drop to the knees and whisper a final prayer. It is in those moments—those quiet, trembling, last-hour pleas—that stories are born. Stories no human being can orchestrate. Stories where the impossible folds in on itself. Stories where God's hand moves with shocking clarity.

For some people, provision is a lesson learned only after every safety net fails. That was the case for Michael and his family. A quiet man in his mid-forties, he was not the sort to raise his hand for help. He carried his burdens like stones in his pockets—silently, privately, determined to shield his wife and children from the weight. He had lost his job four months earlier when the company he'd worked for since college unexpectedly shut down, leaving hundreds unemployed. At first, he reassured his wife, Rachel, that everything would be fine. He had savings. He had experience. He had faith that the right opportunity would open. But weeks turned to months, interviews came and went, and the certainty began to fray around the edges.

By the time winter arrived, the savings were gone. Their mortgage had fallen behind, and the electricity company had sent two warnings stamped in red. The fridge held little more than condiments and a half carton of milk. Michael could feel the tension in the air, the unspoken worry etched into the lines near Rachel's eyes, the way she hesitated before checking the mail, almost bracing herself before she opened the box.

One evening, after the children fell asleep, Michael sat at the dining table in the dark, the only light coming from the streetlamp outside. He laid out the bills—mortgage, electricity, insurance—and added them for the third time that night. The total did not change. His account balance had not miraculously grown. His strength to pretend was thinning. Rachel joined him quietly, sitting across from him without a word. She reached for his hand, her thumb instinctively brushing the back of his knuckles. "We're going to pray," she said softly. "Tonight, we are not praying for the job. We are praying for tomorrow, for whatever God chooses to do."

Michael bowed his head, but for the first time in years, he had no idea what to say. He tried to begin, but the words stalled at the edge of his throat. Rachel squeezed his hand, and the prayer came from her instead—simple, trembling, honest. "Lord, You see us. We're out of answers. We need You. Please meet us in this place. Please provide what we cannot."

When she finished, they sat there in silence, listening to the hum of the refrigerator and the faint whistle of wind against the windows. Michael did not feel a stirring. No warmth. No revelation. No reassurance. Just exhaustion. He rose from his seat, kissed Rachel's forehead, and whispered, "I don't know how much longer we can hold on."

She answered, "God does."

The next morning, Michael tried to stretch the last of their groceries into breakfast. The kids needed to eat before school, but there wasn't much to offer. Rachel managed oatmeal with the last scoop from the container, thinning it with water so everyone could have a small bowl. Michael slipped a spoonful back into the pot when nobody was looking so the children would have more. When they left for school, he kissed them and forced a smile, but one of the girls—his youngest—paused and asked, "Daddy, are you sad today?"

He knelt beside her and brushed her hair behind her ear. "I'm okay," he said. "Just praying."

She nodded, satisfied with that answer, and ran to catch up with her brother.

By noon, the house was cold. Michael lowered the thermostat again, doing anything he could to delay the shutoff he feared was coming. He sent out more job applications, attended another virtual interview that ended with polite promises and empty reassurances, and tried to read Scripture but found himself staring at the same verse repeatedly without absorbing it. Rachel suggested they call their pastor, Pastor Jonah, who had been checking in periodically.

Michael resisted at first—he hated the idea of appearing needy—but he eventually agreed.

When Jonah arrived later that afternoon, he didn't lecture or ask uncomfortable questions. He simply sat down, listened, and placed a hand on Michael's shoulder. "You're not alone," he said quietly. "You've been trying to carry every burden by yourself, but God is not asking you to be the hero of this story. He's asking you to let Him be."

Michael's throat tightened. He nodded, unable to speak.

Jonah prayed with them for provision—not three weeks from now, not next month, but today. "Lord, You know what this family needs," he said. "We trust You. Show us Your hand."

After the pastor left, the house felt strangely still. Michael walked to the mailbox out of habit. Inside was nothing but a coupon booklet and a credit card offer he immediately tore in half. When he came back in, Rachel was cleaning the kitchen counter for the third time that day, wiping it even though it was spotless. He stood behind her, resting his hands on her shoulders, both of them anchoring one another in silence.

The sun dipped lower, painting the living room in amber light. As the clock moved toward evening, Michael could feel the anxiety rising again. They needed food for dinner. They needed money for the mortgage. They needed a miracle—but Michael had grown weary of expecting one.

It was just past six when there was a knock on the front door. Rachel looked up, startled. They weren't expecting anyone. Michael opened the door to find an elderly man from the church—Mr. Wallace—standing on the porch with a paper bag in his hand and a sheepish look on his face.

"Sorry to drop by unannounced," Wallace said, shifting the bag in his arms. "I was at the grocery store earlier, and I felt a strong urge to pick up a few things for you. I don't know why. Maybe I'm losing my mind. But I couldn't shake it."

He handed Michael the bag. Inside were groceries—bread, pasta, vegetables, chicken, fruit, cereal. Enough to last at least a few days. Michael stared down at it, his vision blurring. "How did you—why would you—"

Wallace shrugged awkwardly. "I don't know. I just felt led. Hope it's not too strange."

Rachel stepped forward, tears in her eyes. "Thank you," she whispered. "You have no idea what this means."

Wallace nodded, embarrassed by the emotion. "God puts things on the heart for a reason. You two take care."

When he left, Michael carried the bag into the kitchen and set it on the table. He stood there staring at it, feeling something inside him loosen—something he had kept tightly clenched for months. Rachel hugged him from behind, her face pressed between his shoulder blades. "He heard us," she whispered.

But the miracle wasn't finished.

Fifteen minutes later, there was another knock. This time it was their neighbor—a single mother named Aria who worked long hours. She looked apologetic and held out an envelope. "I'm sorry to bother you," she said, "but I got this by mistake. It was in my mailbox. It has your name on it."

Michael took the envelope, thanked her, and closed the door. He opened it slowly, expecting another bill. Instead, inside was a letter from a company he had applied to months ago. They apologized for the delay in communication due to restructuring but wanted to schedule an immediate follow-up interview—and included a prepaid debit card for travel expenses. The amount on it was $500.

Michael felt his knees weaken. Rachel covered her mouth with her hand, her eyes wide, shimmering. "Michael… that's enough to catch us up for now. That's enough to get through this week."

He held the card as if it were fragile, his breath uneven. "We didn't even ask for this," he said softly, "and God still sent it."

Rachel replied, "We did ask. Last night. We just didn't know how He would answer."

The moments kept unfolding like falling dominoes. After dinner—real dinner, the first full meal they'd had in days—the phone rang.

Jonah's voice came through the speaker. "I hope I'm not calling too late," he said. "I just wanted you to know that during prayer tonight, someone handed me an anonymous donation envelope. They said God put your family on their heart. Michael... the amount is exactly what you need for your mortgage payment."

Michael sat down slowly, pressing a hand to his forehead as tears finally pushed free. Rachel covered her face and sobbed. Jonah continued speaking gently, "I know life has been pressing you on every side. But God hasn't forgotten you. Today proves that."

When they hung up, the house was quiet again. The kind of quiet that settles after a storm finally breaks, when the first ray of sunlight reaches through the clouds. Michael leaned back in his chair and stared at the ceiling—not in disbelief, but in awe.

He thought back to the night before, sitting in the dark with Rachel, praying for tomorrow. He thought about the words that had been so hard to speak, the weight of admitting he had nothing left. He thought about Jonah's reminder: You are not the hero of this story.

God was.

And in that final hour—in the exact moment where they were empty—God filled the gaps. He sent food before the hunger became unbearable. He sent money before the bills suffocated hope. He sent confirmation that He saw them, that every tear, every whispered prayer, every moment of waiting had been heard.

Later that night, as Michael tucked the children into bed, his youngest asked him again, "Daddy, are you sad today?"

He smiled at her—not the forced smile of the morning, but one that reached his eyes fully. "No, sweetheart," he said. "God helped us today."

She nodded as if that made perfect sense. "Because He always helps us," she said matter-of-factly. "You told me that."

Michael kissed her forehead and turned out the light. In the hallway, Rachel slipped her hand into his. They stood there, not speaking, both overwhelmed by the nearness of God.

Provision in the final hour isn't just about

money or groceries or unexpected envelopes. It's about the unmistakable truth that when everything runs out—strength, resources, ideas, dignity—God steps in with a precision that cannot be chalked up to luck, coincidence, or timing.

What happened to Michael's family would be told for years in their church. People would shake their heads and say, "Only God." They would point to the groceries, the envelope, the donation, and say, "This is what it looks like when heaven moves."

But for Michael, it wasn't the things God sent that changed him. It was the realization that he had never been unseen. Never abandoned. Never forgotten. God had been waiting for the moment when his hands were open and empty, ready to receive. And when that moment finally arrived, God poured out more than they asked for, more than they imagined, and far more than they deserved.

Because that is what He does—in the final hour, and every hour in between.

Chapter Fifteen

Everyday Miracles, Extraordinary God

"Most of the miracles God performs will never make the news. They happen quietly, unseen by cameras, unnoticed by crowds, yet they shift the entire direction of a life."

It is easy for people to believe in miracles when a heart restarts after an hour, or a child survives what no doctor can explain. Those moments, dramatic and overwhelming, command attention. But what many miss—what slips by as forgettable, ordinary, or easily explained—is that God often moves in ways so subtle, so gentle, that we don't recognize the miracle until long after it has already passed. Some miracles roar; others whisper. And sometimes, it is the whisper that changes everything.

There is something humbling about the miracles that happen in the minutes between sunrise and sleep—moments no one applauds for, moments not photographed or broadcast, moments only the person involved will remember. These miracles don't always save a life, yet they reshape the heart. They don't always flip the laws of nature, yet they reroute circumstances with a quiet precision that makes a person stop and breathe, aware that something holy just touched their day.

Consider the story of a woman named Elara who woke one morning with a heaviness she could not explain. Nothing was wrong, not in the way a crisis announces itself. But something was pressing against her spirit, something she didn't have words for. As she stood by her kitchen counter, sipping coffee, she whispered a simple prayer—one sentence, spoken softly, not desperate or dramatic: "Lord, if You're trying to tell me something, let me hear You today." She went about her routine, unaware that her simple request had already been answered.

Driving later that afternoon, she approached a familiar intersection where she always turned right. She hesitated without knowing why. A gentle nudge—not audible, not forceful, just a quiet pull in her spirit—told her to wait. And for no logical reason, she did. Five seconds later, a truck sped through the red light at the exact moment she would have been crossing. She sat frozen, realizing that waiting without explanation was the difference between driving home safely and suffering a tragedy. No paramedics were called. No headline appeared. But it was a miracle all the same—a miracle disguised as hesitation, a miracle masked in stillness.

This is the kind of miracle God performs often. Small shifts in timing. Delays that feel inconvenient. Urges to wait a moment longer. A sudden thought that interrupts a pattern. A pause that doesn't make sense in the flesh, yet makes perfect sense in the Spirit.

Another man, Jonah, often worked late at his office. He prided himself on commitment, efficiency, and getting things done. One night, exhausted and irritable, he decided to clock out earlier than usual. It wasn't because he felt God speak, not because he sensed danger. He simply felt tired, and as he packed up his things, he muttered a half-prayer, half-complaint: "Lord, I need rest. That's all I want tonight."

On his drive home he saw someone pulled over on the side of the quiet road, hazard lights blinking in the dim glow of dusk. Normally he would have driven past—too tired, too hungry, too eager to be home—but something tugged at him. Stop.

He argued internally: "Someone else will help. I don't have the energy for this."
 The pull came again. Stop.

He sighed, pulled over, and approached the car. Inside was an elderly woman gripping the steering wheel, trembling. She had been sitting there for almost an hour, terrified to open the door. Her phone was dead, traffic was rare, and she was afraid to step outside in the growing darkness. Jonah helped her get assistance, stayed with her until help arrived, and ensured she got home safely. She grabbed his hand with tears in her eyes and said, "I prayed God would send someone. I didn't know if He heard me."

Jonah drove home quietly, shaken not by what he had done, but by how effortlessly God had woven him into someone else's answer. A tired man leaving work early. A small road. A dying phone. A whisper to stop. No thunder. No dramatic sign. Just provision, orchestrated with stunning simplicity.

Many miracles look like that. A decision we don't understand. A redirection we didn't plan.

A meeting we weren't expecting. A delay that saves us. An interruption that protects us. God is often doing more behind the scenes than we ever imagine.

Some miracles arrive through people we've never met, and others arrive through people who know us deeply. Sometimes they arrive through strangers who feel compelled to speak a sentence that turns out to be exactly what we needed at that exact moment.

There was a young man named Miles who struggled silently with discouragement. He didn't tell anyone—not his parents, not his friends, not even God in prayer. He simply carried the weight, believing it was his burden alone. One afternoon, while sitting at a bus stop, an elderly man next to him looked over with a gentle smile and said, "You don't know this yet, but your story is far from over. You matter more than you think." Miles blinked in shock. He had told no one what he was feeling, yet the very words he needed had been spoken to him by a stranger.

Before he could ask anything—before he could even respond—the man stood and boarded the approaching bus. Miles never saw him again. Years later, he still wondered whether that man was an angel, a messenger, or simply a vessel God used in a crucial moment. But he knew this: God had heard a prayer he never spoke out loud.

Miracles also show up in confirmations—moments when God repeats something in a way too precise to dismiss as coincidence. A woman wrestles with a major decision, asking God for clarity. At church, a sermon touches the exact topic she prayed about that morning. Later that afternoon, a friend calls unexpectedly, speaking words that mirror the thoughts she kept private. That evening, while reading Scripture, she finds the very verse that aligns with everything she heard that day. Each moment could be brushed off as coincidence, but together they form a pattern impossible to ignore. This is how God gently reassures, "I am here. I hear you. I know what you need."

Some miracles are simple but profound—lost items found in impossible places, money showing up at the exact moment a bill is due, strength appearing in a moment of emotional exhaustion. A single sentence from a loved one arrives at the perfect time. A conversation shifts a mindset. A nudge prevents a mistake. A delayed train keeps someone from crossing paths with danger. A sudden urge to pray for someone turns out to be at the exact moment they needed covering.

These are miracles too. God in the details. God in the timing. God in the whisper.

A woman named Kaira once lost her wedding ring. She searched everywhere—rooms, closets, bags, under furniture—with growing panic. That ring held memories she cherished. After an hour of searching, she sat on the floor, closed her eyes, and said quietly, "Lord, You know exactly where it is. Lead me." She stood up, walked into her kitchen without thinking, opened a drawer she had checked twice before, and there it was—sitting in plain sight. The sense of relief washed over her, followed by a quiet awareness that God cared not just about her life, but even about her small anxieties.

Another man sat in his car during his lunch break, feeling the weight of loneliness. He whispered, "Lord, I feel forgotten." Five minutes later, his phone buzzed with a message from a friend he hadn't spoken to in months: "Thinking about you today. You okay?" He stared at the message, overwhelmed. It wasn't a parted sea or a medical wonder. It was a miracle of comfort, a reminder that God sees the quiet ache no one else notices.

One of the most overlooked miracles is peace—true, supernatural peace. Peace that settles over a mind tormented by fear. Peace that quiets a heart unsure about tomorrow. Peace that doesn't match circumstances. It doesn't announce itself with signs or wonders; it simply arrives, steady and sure, like a warm blanket in the cold. Many don't recognize this as a miracle, but it is one of the greatest gifts God gives.

There is also the miracle of protection—tiny near-misses that could have been disastrous but weren't. A toddler slipping yet landing softly. A candle left burning yet causing no fire. A forgotten stove burner that somehow doesn't ignite. A car swerving at the last moment. A distracted step that doesn't lead to injury. Most people shrug these off as luck, but many believers know better. God keeps us from more danger than we will ever see.

A young mother once shared how she forgot to lock her front door one night, something she had never done. She discovered it the next morning, heart pounding. But nothing happened. Her home was untouched. Her family slept peacefully. Something as simple as a forgotten lock became a reminder that God's protection is not limited by our mistakes.

Sometimes the miracle is provision—unexpected, quiet, but exact. A bag of groceries left anonymously on the doorstep. A refund issued out of nowhere. A stranger paying for the meal of someone who barely had enough. A job opening appearing just as finances were running dry. Provision that doesn't come with trumpets or applause, but with perfect timing.

And then there are miracles that happen inside the heart. The miracle of forgiveness that seemed impossible. The miracle of letting go. The miracle of courage appearing at the precise moment it's required. The miracle of finding joy again after a season of heaviness. These are not merely emotions—they are divine movements. Healing that takes place in the unseen.

Many people miss these miracles because they expect God to move in dramatic fashion every time. They look for burning bushes and thunderous voices, forgetting that God often speaks in the quiet. They wait for the extraordinary, not realizing that God rarely stops performing miracles; He simply performs many in ways subtle enough to be overlooked.

The greatest shift comes when a person begins

to see God in the everyday. When they train their heart to look for His fingerprints, miracles become easier to notice. Life begins to feel less random and more intentional. What once felt like coincidence now feels like orchestration. What once seemed insignificant now appears sacred.

And so the chapter stretches far beyond the dramatic moments of divine healing or supernatural rescue. It settles into the truth that miracles are not defined by their size but by the fingerprints of God upon them. They appear in small victories, quiet guidance, gentle comfort, and perfectly timed encouragement. They appear in protection we never knew we needed. They appear in the little things that accumulate into big reminders that God is moving, shaping, guarding, whispering, guiding.

Every day, God is busy with miracles. Some we notice, most we don't. But whether seen or unseen, God is at work in the details, in the timing, in the whispers, in the pauses, in the redirections, in the unexpected kindness, in the protection we didn't realize we needed. And when we look closely enough—when we truly pay attention—we discover that the extraordinary God we serve has never stopped performing miracles.

www.ingramcontent.com/pod-product-compliance
Lightning Source LLC
Chambersburg PA
CBHW031255110426
42743CB00039B/232